# Intelligent Virtual System for Underwater Vehicle Piloting using Unity™

# Intelligent Virtual System for Underwater Vehicle Piloting using Unity™

Cheng Siong Chin

CRC Press
Taylor & Francis Group
Boca Raton London New York

CRC Press is an imprint of the
Taylor & Francis Group, an **informa** business

First edition published 2020
by CRC Press
6000 Broken Sound Parkway NW, Suite 300, Boca Raton, FL 33487-2742

and by CRC Press
2 Park Square, Milton Park, Abingdon, Oxon, OX14 4RN

© 2021 Cheng Siong Chin

CRC Press is an imprint of Taylor & Francis Group, LLC

The right pf Cheng Siong Chin to be identified as author of this work has been asserted by him in accordance with sections 77 and 78 of the Copyright, Designs and Patents Act 1988.

*Library of Congress Cataloging-in-Publication Data*
Names: Chin, Cheng Siong, author.
Title: Intelligent Virtual System for Underwater Vehicle Piloting using Unity / Cheng Siong Chin.
Description: First edition. | Boca Raton, FL : CRC Press, 2021. | Includes bibliographical references and index.
Identifiers: LCCN 2020037238 (print) | LCCN 2020037239 (ebook) | ISBN 9780367653941 (hardback) | ISBN 9781003129288 (ebook)
Subjects: LCSH: Autonomous underwater vehicles. | Remote submersibles. | Intelligent control systems. | Unity (Electronic resource)
Classification: LCC VM365 .C475 2021 (print) | LCC VM365 (ebook) | DDC 623.82/05--dc23
LC record available at https://lccn.loc.gov/2020037238
LC ebook record available at https://lccn.loc.gov/2020037239

ISBN: 978-0-367-65394-1 (hbk)
ISBN: 978-1-003-12928-8 (ebk)

Typeset in Palatino
by codeMantra

# *Contents*

Preface......................................................................................................... vii
Acknowledgments ...................................................................................... ix
Author........................................................................................................ xiii

**1. Introduction to Unity™** ...................................................................... 1
   1.1   Introduction ................................................................................ 1
   1.2   Comparison of Different Game Engines ................................. 5
   1.3   Overall View of Unity3D Framework ..................................... 7
   1.4   Author Publications .................................................................. 8
   References ........................................................................................... 8

**2. Development of ROV's Pilot Training Platform Using Unity™**.... 13
   2.1   Proposed Methodology Using Unity™ ..................................... 13
   2.2   Overall Software Structure........................................................ 13
   2.3   Unity's Configurations and Setups ......................................... 15
   2.4   Unity™ Editor Interface ............................................................ 15
   2.5   Installation of Unity™ ............................................................... 17
   2.6   Create New Project .................................................................... 19
   2.7   Developing Virtual Environment............................................. 20
       2.7.1   Virtual Seabed .............................................................. 21
       2.7.2   Importing of Subsea 3D Models ................................. 27
       2.7.3   Environment Lighting.................................................. 36
       2.7.4   Underwater Particles ................................................... 40
   2.8   ROV Model and Specification ................................................. 43
   2.9   Configuration of TRV-M in Virtual Simulation..................... 45
   2.10  Controller Input......................................................................... 57
   2.11  Data Logging ............................................................................. 62
   2.12  Graphic User Interface (GUI).................................................... 62
   2.13  Scripting ..................................................................................... 65
       2.13.1  RovControl.................................................................... 65
       2.13.2  SwitchCamera............................................................... 69
       2.13.3  Manipulators ................................................................ 71
       2.13.4  Spotlight........................................................................ 73
       2.13.5  Timer Script .................................................................. 73
       2.13.6  DataLogger ................................................................... 74
       2.13.7  ButtonScript................................................................. 76

**3. Results and Discussion** ........................................................................ 81
   3.1    Virtual Simulation Results with Videos ...................................... 81
   3.2    User Experience Study of ROV Pilot Simulator......................... 86
        3.2.1   Participants ........................................................................ 86
        3.2.2   ROV Pilot Situational Performance.............................. 87
   3.3    Questionnaire............................................................................... 87

**4. Conclusion**........................................................................................... 93

**Appendix A: TRV-M ROV Technical Specification Sheet** .................... 95

**Appendix B: Functions of the Properties Used in Unity™** .................... 97

**Appendix C: Joystick Software Installation** .......................................... 105

**Appendix D: Scripts** ................................................................................113

**Index**...................................................................................................... 137

# *Preface*

Virtual reality (VR) simulation of an underwater vehicle is defined as human immersion in VR to simulate systems in a complex environment using the software. VR simulator can mimic a complicated activity in the real world. The VR simulator using an open-source game engine such as Unity™ and a mobile head-mounted display can increase mobility, improve the human–machine interaction, and decrease the development time and cost. The primary element in carrying out underwater missions in a hostile environment lies within the skills and experience of a human pilot. Training is always essential to prevent damage to expensive field equipment during real operations. The proposed simulator differs from the existing simulators in the market in the use of the modern game engine to develop a "serious game" for the underwater vehicle (or even aerospace) pilot trainee with minimal cost. Hence, in this book, the user study of VR simulation results revealed that the proposed virtual simulator software using Unity™ game engine could replicate the pilot training with compatible user's experience for the subsea operation when compared to commercial software. The book allows researchers and students to explore and test different control schemes on the same platform.

This book has been prepared for the needs of those who seek an application on developing VR simulation for an underwater vehicle where the actual physical prototype is not available during the initial design stage. Also, some software is difficult to understand, and details on how to obtain the model can be missing. It often impedes the process of simulation. The book can be used as a reference book for undergraduate and postgraduate, engineers, researchers, and lecturers in VR simulation using Unity™ as the leading software. The sample codes used in this book are provided to aid in your learning. Unity™ programming code is also available as an e-resource on the CRC Press website: www.routledge.com/9780367653941.

# Acknowledgments

Finally, I wish to acknowledge my great debt to all those who have contributed to the development of simulation into the field it is today, specifically to the considerable help and education I have received from my final-year project days in Nanyang Technological University (NTU) with Dr Michael Lau Wai Shing and Dr Eicher Low. I would first like to thank my late master thesis advisor Professor Neil Munro, who had made control engineering alive by using computer-aided software. I had benefited from his knowledge in the robust control and the computer-aided control engineering. Without his enthusiasm, I won't have pursued my doctorate study. Lastly, I would like to thank the editorial staff and reviewers for providing comments to the text. The programming codes and graphical diagrams are provided in this book.

I would like to always express my gratefulness to my family. In particular, I would like to thank Irene (my wife), Giselle (my late elder daughter), Millicent (my second daughter), Tessalyn (my third daughter), and Alyssa (my youngest daughter) for their support and understanding, without which the undertaking would not have been possible. I would like to share my joy and results with my strong and kind daughter, Giselle. Her persistence eventually wore her down, and she passed away at the age of four years after a few consecutive open-heart surgeries. Without her presence and attitude towards life, many things would not happen. I couldn't have survived until now. I have collected all my tears and preserved them into this book to continue my academic journey and turn that sadness into strength. I hope to encourage more collaborative research no matter who and where you are.

**Professor Cheng Siong Chin**
*Ph.D., M.Sc., B.Eng., Dip.Mech.*
*FHEA, FIMarEST, SMIEEE, Eur Ing, MIET, CEng,*
*Newcastle University, Singapore*
*Adjunct Professor to Chongqing University, China*

## OUTLINES

The contents of the book are organized into four main chapters with programming codes and graphical diagrams. The main chapters include a section on the proposed methodology used for virtual reality (VR) simulator. In these chapters, it contains applications using Unity™ on the various subsystems required in the virtual environment for remotely operated vehicle (ROV). As it is not possible to cover all different application scenarios, the book, therefore, emphasizes applications such as subsea pipeline inspection. The ROV pilot will be asked to complete the underwater pipeline inspection for leakage and subsequently tasked to shut down the system to prevent further oil leakage in a given time frame. The trainee can repeatedly practice under some challenge-driven practices such as to reduce the total operation time and distance traveled for the entire mission.

Although there are many underwater vehicle simulators available in today's market, the cost to design and implement the ROV pilot simulator is quite high. Moreover, the developed simulation system could require a good knowledge of programming languages for software maintenance. Besides, the current commercial system requires the user interface or console to be mounted on the floor which has always limited the mobility of the system. Fortunately, the advances in consumer electronics such as mobile head-mounted display and VR improve the mobility and the human–machine interaction. However, the existing ROV pilot training simulators suggest the need for a new approach to the high fidelity simulation. A fun and engaging game improves the time and cost to market further, mobility on ROV pilot training, and the training experience of users.

Hence, a serious game-based approach to improve learning experience is desired. Unity 3D game engine has been widely used in robot applications. The software adopted throughout the chapters is Unity™. The codes can be downloaded from the website: https://drive.google.com/drive/fold ers/1qb74vzBIeC5hdhm66amu4nXw5WYxtx4q?usp=sharing.

The chapters are written in a coherent manner, where each chapter is closely connected. This allows the readers to understand the entire process from modeling to VR simulation.

Chapter 1: Introduction to VR simulation
Chapter 2: Proposed methodology used for VR simulator
Chapter 3: Overall software structure for VR simulator

Chapter 4: Unity's configurations and setup includes interface, installation, virtual environment, 3D models, environment lighting, configuration in virtual simulation, controller input, data logging, scripting, and camera. The recorded videos of the completed virtual simulator performing the tasks can be seen on the following websites:

- Setup: https://www.youtube.com/watch?v=vIjLfBF3soo
- Training: https://www.youtube.com/watch?v=PNyD1qRLCYU

# *Author*

**Dr. Cheng Siong Chin** received a B.Eng. in Mechanical and Production Engineering from Nanyang Technological University (NTU) in 2000, a M.Sc. in Advanced Control and Systems Engineering from The University of Manchester (formerly called UMIST), UK, in 2001, and a Ph.D. in Research Robotics Centre, NTU, in 2008. He is currently a reader (associate professor) with Newcastle University and an adjunct full professor in the School of Automotive Engineering at the Chongqing University. He has published over 100 publications, 4 books, and 3 US patents. His research interests include the design and simulation of complex systems for an uncertain environment. He is a fellow of the Higher-Education Academy, fellow of IMarEST, senior member of IEEE and the IET, and a chartered engineer. In 2018, he was invited as a plenary speaker and chief guest to the IEEE International Conference on Power, Energy Control and Transmission Systems in India. He served as a lead guest editor for the *Journal of Advanced Transportation* (Special Issue on Intelligent Autonomous Transport Systems Design and Simulation) and organizer for Special Session on Smart and Intelligent Controller-Based Grid Integration of Renewable Energy Systems in IEEE TENCON 2019. He was also involved as the general chair and the technical review committee member for various international conferences (ICRAI 2019 in NTU) related to intelligent systems. Dr. Chin was the panel member and senior member of IEEE Application in Region 10 in 2014 and 2017. He received the Best Paper Award for Virtual Reality of Autonomous Marine Vehicle in 10th International Conference on Modelling, Identification, and Control sponsored by IEEE in 2018 and the Best Application Paper on Dynamic Positioning for Vessel in 11th International Conference on Modelling, Identification, and Control in 2019. He also received the DCASE2019 Judges' Award (most innovative and original) for Sound Event Detection in Domestic Environments in the IEEE AASP Challenge on DCASE2019 with his Ph.D. student. He received the Outstanding Contributions in Reviewing for Future Generation Computer Systems award, Elsevier, in 2018. He is also the associate editor for IEEE *Earthzine* (marine power and battery systems) and *Electronics* (Sections: Systems & Control Engineering and Artificial Intelligence Circuits and Systems), MDPI.

# 1

# *Introduction to Unity™*

## 1.1 Introduction

The demand for remotely operated vehicles (ROVs) [1] has increased extensively over the years due to their ability to carry out a search operation in environments that are beyond human capabilities. With advanced technologies, these underwater vehicles can travel more than 3000 m deep into the ocean for pipeline inspection and cable laying, making them a valuable asset for the offshore industry. The ROV controlled by a pilot on board a vessel relies on limited data received from underwater sensors. Hence, operating the ROV in an uncertain underwater environment is quite challenging for novice pilots who have little experience and knowledge. Moreover, it puts the ROV and surrounding equipment and environment at a higher risk [2]. Although a high level of skills is required for operating the ROV, pilot training is still conducted on-the-job basis [3]. A safe alternative to using a simulated-based pilot training system [3–5] was used. Based on the ROV mission requirements, various operating conditions and vehicle configurations can be constructed in the virtual world [6–7]. Pilot trainees can pick up skills and knowledge in a safe, conducive and low-pressure learning environment assisted with training guides [8].

Following Det Norske Veritas (DNV) standard [9] for maritime simulator systems for ROV operation, there are three levels of performance capabilities for ROV simulators. They are

- ROV Class A (a full mission that is capable of simulating a realistic physics engine and creates an accurate visual representation with a fit for purpose graphics engine)
- ROV Class B (multi-task that can simulate a quasi-realistic physics engine and creates a suitable visual representation)
- ROV Class C (limited task where the performance is defined on a case by case basis).

The Class A simulators provide a higher visual fidelity with an actual environment interface as compared to Class B and C simulators. As a result, there are different types of simulation software available in the market that provide advanced simulated-based training for commercial ROV operators. The current list of simulation software for ROV is not intended to be exhaustive. For example, Offshore Simulator Centre (OSC), DeepWorks ROV by Fugro [10], ROVsim² Pro by Marine Simulation [11], Virtual ROV (VROV) by GRI Simulations [12], UnderWater SIMulator (UWSim) [13], Kelpie [14], and $CO_3$-AUVs [15] are quite commonly used. These simulators offer a broad range of mission configurations with high accuracy of physics simulation, open source or freely available to the developer, and support external sensor interface and graphic simulation. Table 1.1 shows the application and main features of different simulation platforms.

Although there are many ROV or underwater vehicle simulators available in today's market, as shown in Table 1.1, the cost to design and implement the ROV pilot simulator is quite high. Moreover, the developed simulation system could require a good knowledge of programming languages for software maintenance. Besides, the current commercial system requires the user interface or console to be mounted on the floor which has always limited the mobility of the system. Fortunately, the advances in consumer electronics such as mobile head-mounted displays, virtual reality (VR) Gear, Oculus Rift, and Vive improve the mobility and the human–machine interaction. A detailed comparison of various head-mounted displays for VR can be found in the following reference [16–19]. A joystick (Logitech Extreme 3D Pro Joystick) will be used. It is selected

**TABLE 1.1**

Applications and Features of Different Commercial Simulators for ROV and Marine Vehicles

| Simulation Software | Applications | Features |
|---|---|---|
| Offshore Simulator Centre (OSC) | • ROV simulator<br>• Crane simulator<br>• Onshore mission control | • Use graphics engine (Unity3D)<br>• New real physics engine<br>• Subsea integrated simulator |
| DeepWorks | • ROV operator training<br>• Tooling development<br>• Deployment rehearsal | • Full sonar simulation<br>• Pilot training metrics<br>• Advanced hydraulic and electric ROV components<br>• Console and vessel integration option |

*(Continued)*

**TABLE 1.1 (*Continued*)**

Applications and Features of Different Commercial Simulators for ROV and Marine Vehicles

| Simulation Software | Applications | Features |
|---|---|---|
| ROVsim² Pro | • Near shore, coastal, and inland marine operation training | • Integration of scanning SONAR simulator<br>• Variety of ROV tool<br>• Wide range of mission scenarios<br>• Originated from video game industry |
| Virtual ROV | • Mission planning and rehearsal<br>• Search and recovery<br>• Military<br>• Control system design support | • Provides high fidelity of dynamic interaction<br>• Provides a broad range of ROV tooling<br>• Able to simulate complex operation |
| UWSim | • Underwater vehicles with/without robotic manipulators<br>• Surface vessels simulator | • Open-source supporting Robotic Operating System (ROS) framework, Blender rendering, and OpenSceneGraph (OSG)<br>• Multiple-ROV simulation<br>• Simulated sensors<br>• Support physics simulation<br>• Network interfaces<br>• Support for customizable widgets |
| Kelpie | • Multi-robot<br>• Water surface and aerial vehicles<br>• Surface vessels simulator | • Open-source backed by OSG, OSG-Ocean library, OpenGL (Open Graphical Language), and ROS<br>• Provide physics engine using Bullet Physics software development kit (SDK) |
| CO₃-AUVs | • Robot<br>• Underwater vehicles | • Open-source integrated with Unified System for Automation and Robot Simulation (USARSim)<br>• Provide physics engine using Bullet Physics SDK<br>• Use Open-Source 3D Graphics Engine (OGRE) as the rendering engine |
| VMAX ROV Simulator | • Underwater vehicles<br>• Surface vessel simulator<br>• Crane simulator | • Include asset integrity management software<br>• Include tether management and multi-function manipulator |

due to its cost, availability, and compatibility with the most software platform and strong online support communities that allow the development of VR applications. Efforts to find an appropriate adjunctive to conventional training methods have led the ROV training community to use simulation and VR for training novice ROV pilots. The applications like these show how different inequalities in ROV pilot training can be solved with VR displayed on VR device. However, the existing ROV pilot training simulators suggest the need for a new approach to the high fidelity simulation and fun and engaging games [20] improve the time and cost to market further.

Hence, a serious game-based approach [21–23] to improve the learning experience is desired. The origin of serious games is not very clear [24]. However, what is essential is the advantages of using the game approach as compared to the traditional VR simulation training. The serious game approach enables the ability for the user to practice repeatedly, provide feedback to action, and offer competitive challenge-driven practice in a fun and engaging manner. The challenge-driven serious games can be applied where the repeated practice is necessary to enhance decision-making skills for real-life tasks in underwater. Recently, a book was published on the serious game on different VR and game applications [25] in the areas of medical training, emotion assessment, music education, gamification, teaching, and learning in schools.

For example, Unity3D game engine was used in robot applications [22]; the Blender open-source 3D modeling toolkit and the game engine were applied to defense technology such as mine detection [26], the academic prototype of 3D Virtual Operating Room project (3DVOR) was used in surgical training [27], and KIDI and BitBox! were used in teaching [28] and gamification of Cognitive Bias Modification (i.e., CityBuilder game) for childhood education [29]. However, the serious game approach in the area of ROV pilot training suffered from a low immersion of researchers working in this field, thus resulting in less literature for references.

The time and cost to market and mobility on ROV pilot training can be resolved by using mobile wearable devices such as Gear VR and the open-source software for serious game development. However, the training experience of users can be affected by the types of the game engine used. There exist a few popular open-source game engine software such as Unity3D [22], Unreal Engine 4 [29], and CryEngine [30–32] available for wide users. The list of game engines shown in this book is not intended to be exhaustive. It is not possible to create the ROV pilot training in a few different types of game engines due to manpower resources and limitations. Instead, the Unity3D [22] was chosen. In the proposed design of VR using the Unity3D game engine, information can be displayed as a back story that describes the ROV's working environment or scene near to the seabed coupled with control information for the maneuverability of ROV through the guides on a display screen. The ROV pilot [33] will be asked to complete the underwater pipeline inspection for leakage and subsequently tasked to shut down the system to prevent further oil leakage in a given time frame. Recorded information such as ROV's position, the total operation time for the entire operation, the status of manipulators, and the view of the ROV allows an instant view of information. The stored training data allow ROV's pilot trainees to review their performance after the training session and for scoring purposes. The trainee can repeatedly practice under some challenge-driven practice such as to reduce the total operation time and distance traveled for the entire mission despite facing the obstacles and a different starting position on the seabed.

In summary, this book contributes to the growing evidence supporting the development of ROV pilot training simulators by exploiting open-source gaming software and the importance of using established and widely available games design techniques in providing engaging scenarios for the ROV training developers and trainees. The control of ROV using a simple and publicly available gaming controller such as a game joystick (to move the ROV) on a standard laptop instead of a powerful workstation reduces the time and development cost. Besides, it improves the system's mobility and the user's experience for the ROV community.

Unity™ is a 3D and 2D game-making tool. Sometimes, it is called "Unity 3D" as it could be a reference to the 3D part of the tool. Alternatively, it can be called Unity 5 that refers to a certain version of Unity3D. In this book, Unity3D, Unity™, and Unity 5 are used interchangeably.

The gamification of ROV pilot training can enhance learning in ROV control through feedback. Serious games have a significant role in a critical task as serious games provide a chance for training until a certain level of expertise is achieved. Besides, immediate feedback in learning and intrinsic scoring in serious games improve their skills.

## 1.2 Comparison of Different Game Engines

There exists a few open-source game engine software that provides excellent features and developing tools. Some of the common characters of a game engine are rendering, physics (2D and 3D rigidbody), scripting, audio, and animation. Depending on the requirements, these game engine software uses traditional programming method that requires basic coding to high-level sandbox engine that provides "drag and drops" interface. The main objective is to simulate an ROV operation using a high-level sandbox game engine for the ease of usability. The options are more toward the sandbox engine and the more common software for game development such as Unity™, Unreal Engine 4, and CryEngine 3.

Unity3D was first released in 2005. It uses mostly JavaScript or C# or managed code toolchain that makes it simpler to support and develop new workflows and instruments. It has large supporting communities that include the asset store for downloading different game characters, particles, and sound effects. Due to its popularity, there exists a good educational material and large active user. However, the free version of Unity™ does not have a Profiler that allows the programmer to optimize the game and check the time spent on rendering and animation during the game. Unity3D supports around 21 platforms as compared to Unreal Engine 4 with only around six platforms. In addition, the 3D models in Unity3D can simply import as game assets into the software, thus improving the efficiency of development.

Unreal Engine was first released in 1998. It provides developers with powerful tools such as access to full source code, simulate and immerse view, persona animation, and cascade visual effects. It is used in a custom workstation with a better and optimized performance that implies higher cost and complexity. Unreal has much larger download than Unity3D as it requires a visual studio for its programming environment and accepts only C++ development language. Unreal Engine can produce high-quality graphics with advanced dynamic lightings, making it a plus point for the game engine. However, the script used in Unreal Engine 4 can only be written in C++ that can be a drawback for beginners. Similar to Unity3D, Unreal Engine 4 has an asset store to download different game assets. However, the user community is not as large as Unity3D.

CryEngine started in 2002. It is another modern game engine that provides excellent features that will create great realistic gameplay. With its pixel-accurate displacement mapping, it allows developers to craft and modify a game as precise as possible to its finest detail. Its excellent graphic capabilities exceed those in Unity3D and Unreal Engine. However, a drawback from this game engine is that it requires a slightly higher learning curve before one can use the game engine efficiently, and it may be harder for those with no game development background.

Notably, these three game engines provide great features for the most development process. It can be entirely subjective in the selection decision. Depending on the development objectives and requirements, one may pick Unity3D for its capabilities in developing 2D and 3D games, Unreal Engine for its powerful tools, or CryEngine for its extreme graphics capabilities. Fortunately, these game engines are freely available for education and research except for Unity3D that requires Pro version for advanced features. On the other hand, the Unreal Engine and CryEngine require a slightly higher learning curve, posing difficulty for most beginners. Based on the following guidelines, the free version of Unity3D that contains most of the functions will be used in developing a simulator for ROV pipeline tracking as it is easy to use, free of research purpose, and the presence of vast user community. It may not be the best choice for every programmer, but during the development of the VR simulator, there are no significant problems encountered, and hence, the option supported by the functions was good enough.

- Able to communicate with external hardware
- Ease to program and use graphical user interface for controlling interaction and animating objects
- Able to process multimedia sensory data
- Free to use for education and research
- Able to hold multiple operating systems
- Able to support development with a strong developer community.

## 1.3 Overall View of Unity3D Framework

The framework of Unity3D is split into three different components: the engine, Editor, and distribution modules. Figure 1.1 shows an idea of a GameObject consisting of separate components that will blend and make up an environment. Any settings that require modifying (e.g., coordinates of the underwater vehicle) are through the component's variable. The overall idea of a GameObject structure is a highlight in Figure 1.1. Every scene consists of a hierarchy that compromises all the GameObject that may be direct asset files like 3D models. Therefore, a typical game can include one

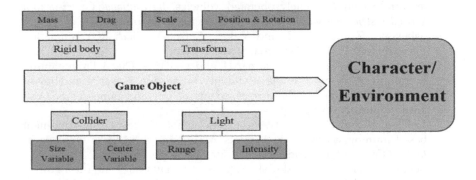

**FIGURE 1.1**
GameObject with components added to form game environment in Unity3D.

or several scenes. When a particular GameObject is a parent, all its movement and rotation will be mimicked by its child. After coupling all the required components to a GameObject, scripting is required to trigger the game scene or to modify the properties of a component during the development phase. Scripts can be considered to be one of the components of a GameObject which can be easily created in Unity3D.

## 1.4  Author Publications

Throughout these few years, I have published around 27 peer-reviewed publications and books as mainly first [33–59] and corresponding authors in the areas of modelling and simulation of underwater systems such as ROV and autonomous underwater vehicle (AUV). It is important to share the research to interested communities and practitioners to help one another to reduce the time to learn the simulated-based system.

## References

1. Christ, R. and Wernli Sr, R. (2014), The ROV Manual, Second Edition: A User Guide for Remotely Operated Vehicles, *Ocean News & Technology*, 20(1), pp. 76–76.
2. Brutzman, D. (1995), Virtual world visualization for an autonomous underwater vehicle, *MTS/IEEE OCEANS '95 Challenges of Our Changing Global Environment*, San Diego, California, U.S.A., pp. 1592–1600.
3. Pioch, N.J., Roberts, B. and Zeltzer, D. (1997), A virtual environment for learning to pilot remotely operated vehicles, *International Conference on Virtual Systems and MultiMedia*, Geneva, Switzerland, pp. 218–226.
4. Fabeković, Z., Eškinja, Z. and Vukić, Z. (2007), Micro ROV simulator, *Proceedings ELMAR*, Zadar, Croatia, pp. 97–101.
5. Alexander, A.L., Brunyé, T., Sidman, J. and Weil, S.A. (2005), From gaming to training: A review of studies on fidelity, immersion, presence, and buy-in and their effects on transfer in pc-based simulations and games, DARWARS Training Impact Group, 5, p. 14.
6. Fletcher, B. and Harris, S. (1996), Development of a virtual environment based training system for ROV pilots, *MTS/IEEE OCEANS'96 Prospects for the 21st Century*, Fort Lauderdale, Florida, U.S.A, pp. 65–71.
7. Bell, B., Kanar, A. and Kozlowski, S. (2008), Current issues and future directions in simulation- based training in North America, *International Journal of Human Resource Management*, 19(8), pp. 1416–1434.

8. IMCA (2015), Guidance on the Use of Simulators, International Marine Contractors Association. https://rules.dnvgl.com/docs/pdf/DNV/std-cert/2011-01/Standard2-14.pdf, assessed 12 May 2020.
9. Fugro (2011), DeepWorks: Complete Mission Simulation and Visualisation, https://www.subseauk.com/documents/fssl%20ssuk%20ucl%202013.pdf, assessed 12 May 2020.
10. MarineSimulation (2011), ROVsim2 Pro. http://www.marinesimulation. com/Public/ROVsim2%20Pro%20Flyer.pdf, assessed 12 May 2020.
11. Simulation, G. (2015), Virtual Remotely Operated Vehicle Simulator. http:// www.grisim.com/wp-content/uploads/2015/01/Product-Brochure.pdf, assessed 12 May 2020.
12. Zyda, M. (2005), From visual simulation to virtual reality to games, *Computer*, 38(9), pp. 25–32.
13. Prats, M., P´erez, J., Javier Fern´andez, J. and Sanz, P.J. (2012), An open source tool for simulation and supervision of underwater, intervention missions, *2012 IEEE/RSJ International Conference on Intelligent Robots and Systems*, October 7–12, Vilamoura, Algarve, Portugal, pp. 2577–2582.
14. Mendonça, R., Santana, P., Marques, F., Lourenço, A., Silva, J. and Barata, J. (2013), Kelpie: A ROS-based multi-robot simulator for water surface and aerial vehicles. In *Proceedings of the IEEE International Conference on Systems, Man, and Cybernetics (SMC)*, Washington, DC, USA, pp. 3645–3650.
15. Birk, A., Antonelli, G., Pascoal, A. and Caffaz, A. (2010), Cognitive cooperative control for autonomous underwater vehicles: An overview of achievements in the first project year, *9th International Conference on Computer Applications and Information Technology in the Maritime Industries (COMPIT)*, Gubbio, Italy, pp.1–16.
16. Buña, P., Górskia, F., Wichniareka, R., Kuczkoa, W., Hamrola, A. and Zawadzkia, P. (2015), Application of professional and low-cost head mounted devices in immersive educational application, *Procedia Computer Science*, 75, pp. 173–181.
17. Miller, J., Baiotto, H., MacAllister, A., Hoover, M., Evans, G., Schlueter, J., Kalivarapu, V. and Winer, E. (2017), Comparison of a virtual game-day experience on varying devices, *Electronic Imaging*, 2017(16), pp. 30–37.
18. Pulijala, Y., Ma, M. and Ayoub, A. (2017), *VR Surgery: Interactive Virtual Reality Application For Training Oral And Maxillofacial Surgeons Using Oculus Rift and Leap Motion. Serious Games and Edutainment Applications*. Volume II, Springer International Publishing, Switzerland, 187–202.
19. Hussein, M. and Nätterdal, C. The benefits of virtual reality in education a comparison study, *Bachelor of Science Thesis in Software Engineering and Management*, Chalmers University of Technology and University of Gothenburg, Göteborg, Sweden, June 2015.
20. Graafland, M., et al. (2012), Systematic review of serious games for medical education and surgical skills training, *British Journal of Surgery*, 99(10), pp. 1322–1330.
21. Jingming, X. (2012), Research on key technologies base Unity3D game engine', *7th International Conference on Computer Science & Education (ICCSE)*, Melbourne, Australia, pp. 695–699.

22. Bartneck, C., Soucy, M., Fleuret, K. and Sandoval, E.B. (2015), The robot engine - Making the unity 3D game engine work for HRI, *Proceedings of the IEEE International Symposium on Robot and Human Interactive Communication (RO-MAN2015)*, Kobe, pp. 431–437.
23. Michael, D.R. and Chen, S.L. (2005), *Serious Games: Games that Educate, Train, and Inform. Muska & Lipman/Premier-Trade.* https://dl.acm.org/doi/book/10.5555/1051239
24. Djaouti, D., Alvarez, J., Jessel, J.P. and Rampnoux, O. (2011), Origins of serious games. In: *Serious Games and Edutainment Applications*, Springer, London/New York, 25–43.
25. Ma, M. and Oikonomou, A. (eds.) (2017), *Serious Games and Edutainment Applications.* Volume II, Springer International Publishing, Switzerland.
26. Stone, R., Snell, T. and Cooke, N. (2016), An inexpensive underwater mine countermeasures simulator with real-time 3D after action review, *Defence Technology*, 12(5), 367–379.
27. Panzoli, D., Lelardeux, C.P., Michel, G., Lagarrigue, P., Minville, V. and Lubrano, V. (2017), *Interaction and Communication in an Immersive Learning Game: The Challenges of Modelling Real-Time Collaboration in a Virtual Operating Room, Serious Games and Edutainment Applications.* Volume II, Springer International Publishing, Switzerland, 147–186.
28. McAlpine, K.B. (2017), *Shake and Create: Reappropriating Video Game Technologies for the Enactive Learning of Music, Serious Games and Edutainment Applications.* Volume II, Springer International Publishing, Switzerland, 77–97.
29. Liu, T., Ma, M., Liu, Z., Kim, G.J., Liu, C. and Geng, Q. (2017), *Intelligent Behaviors of Virtual Characters in Serious Games for Child Safety Education, Serious Games and Edutainment Applications.* Volume II, Springer International Publishing, Switzerland, 289–321.
30. Altabel (2015), Altabel Group's Blog Unreal Engine 4, Unity, Cry Engine: What to Choose? https://altabel.wordpress.com/2015/01/22/unreal-engine-4-unity-cry-engine-what-to-choose/, assessed 12 May 2020.
31. Juarez, A., Schonenberg, W. and Bartneck, C. (2010, December), Implementing a low-cost CAVE system using the CryEngine2, *Entertainment Computing*, 1(3–4), pp. 157–164.
32. Schlueter, J., Baiotto, H., Hoover, M., Kalivarapu, V., Evans, G. and Winer, E. (2017), Best practices for cross-platform virtual reality development, *Proceedings Volume 10197, Degraded Environments: Sensing, Processing, and Display 2017*, Anaheim, California, United States.
33. Chin, C.S., Kamsani, N.B., Zhong, X.H., Cui, R. and Yang, C. (2018), Unity3D serious game engine for high fidelity virtual reality training of remotely-operated vehicle pilot, *10th International Conference on Modelling, Identification and Control*, Guiyang, China, 2–4 Jul 2018.
34. Chin, C.S. (2017), Computer-Aided Control Systems Design: Practical Applications Using MATLAB® and Simulink®. (CRC Press, Florida).
35. Eslami, M., Chin, C.S. and Nobakhti, A. (2019), Robust modelling, sliding-mode controller and simulation of an underactuated ROV under parametric uncertainties and disturbance, *Journal of Marine Science and Application*, 18(2), pp. 213–227.

36. Chin, C.S. (2018), Embedded Mechatronics System Design for Uncertain Environments: Linux-based, MATLAB xPC Target, PIC, Arduino and Raspberry Pi Approaches. (IET Press, London).

37. Chin, C.S. and Lin, W.P. (2018), Robust genetic algorithm and fuzzy inference mechanism embedded in sliding-mode controller for uncertain underwater robot, *IEEE/ASME Transactions on Mechatronics*, 32(2), pp. 655–666.

38. Chin, C.S., Lin, W.P. and Lin, J.Y. (2018), Experimental validation of open-frame ROV model for Virtual Reality Simulation and Control, *Journal of Marine Science and Technology*, 23(2), pp. 267–287.

39. Lin, W.P. and Chin, C.S. (2017), Block diagonal dominant remotely-operated vehicle model simulation using decentralized model predictive control, *Advances in Mechanical Engineering (SS: Advanced Intelligent Control of Autonomous Systems)*, 9(4), pp. 1–24.

40. Thekkedan, M.D., Chin, C.S. and Woo, W.L. (2015), Virtual reality simulation of fuzzy-logic control during underwater dynamic positioning, *Journal of Marine Science and Application*, 14(1), pp. 14–24.

41. Lin, W.P., Chin, C.S., Looi, L.C.W., Lim, J.J. and Teh, E.M.E. (2015), Robust design of docking hoop for recovery of autonomous underwater vehicle with experimental results, *Robotics*, 4(4), pp. 492–515.

42. Wan, D. and Chin, C.S. (2015), Simulation and prototype testing of a low-cost ultrasonic distance measurement device in underwater, *Journal of Marine Science and Technology*, 20(1), pp. 142–154.

43. Si, J.T. and Chin, C.S. (2014), An adaptable walking-skid for seabed ROV under strong current disturbance, *Journal of Marine Science and Application*, 13(3), pp. 305–314.

44. Chin, C.S. and Lau, M.S.W. (2012), Modeling and testing of hydrodynamic damping model for a complex-shaped remotely-operated vehicle for control, *Journal of Marine Science and Application*, 11(2), pp. 150–163.

45. Chin, C.S. and Lum, S.H. (2011), Rapid modeling and control systems prototyping of a marine robotic vehicle with model uncertainties using xPC Target System, *Ocean Engineering*, 38(17–18), pp. 2128–2141.

46. Chin, C.S., Lau, M.W.S. and Low, E. (2010), Supervisory cascaded controllers design: Experiment test on a remotely-operated vehicle, Proc, *IMechE Part C: Journal of Mechanical Engineering Science*, 225(3), pp. 584–603.

47. Chin, C. S., Lau, M.W.S., Low, E. and Seet, G.G.L. (2008), Robust and decoupled cascaded control system of the underwater robotic vehicle for stabilization and pipeline tracking, *Proc. IMechE Part I: Journal of Systems and Control Engineering*, 222(4), pp. 261–278.

48. Eng, Y.H., Lau, W.S., Low, E., Seet, G.G.L. and Chin, C.S. (2008), Estimation of the hydrodynamic coefficients of an ROV using Free Decay Pendulum Motion, *Engineering Letters*, 16(3), pp. 326–331.

49. Chin, C.S., Lau, M.W.S., Low, E. and Seet, G.G.L. (2006), Dynamic Modelling and Cascaded Controller Design of a Low-Speed Maneuvering ROV, Advanced Technologies: Research, Development and Application Book, pp. 159–186. (Advanced Robotic Systems International, Pro Literatur Verlag.

50. Chin, C.S., Lau, M.W.S., Low, E. and Seet, G.G.L. (2006), Software for modelling and simulation of a remotely operated vehicle, *International Journal of Simulation Modeling*, 5(3), pp. 114–125.

51. Chin, C.S., Lau, M.W.S., Low, E. and Seet, G.G.L. (2006), Robust controller design method and stability analysis of an underactuated underwater vehicle, *International Journal of Applied Mathematics and Computer Science*, 16(3), pp. 101–112.
52. Lin, W.P. and Chin, C.S. (2014) Remote Underwater Dual Cameras Video Image Acquisition System using Linux Based Embedded PC104, OCEANS'14 MTS/IEEE, Taipei, pp. 1–6.
53. Lin, W.P. and Chin, C.S. (2014), Remote Robust Control and Simulation of Robot for Search and Rescue Mission in Water, OCEANS'14 MTS/IEEE, Taipei, pp. 1–9.
54. Chin, C.S. Lau, M.W.S., Tan, Y.J., Chee, K.F. and Wong, Y.C. (2009), Development, and Testing of an AUV using industrial xPC-Target Platform, IEEE/ASME International Conference on Advanced Intelligent Mechatronics, Singapore , pp. 1076–1081.
55. Eng, Y.H., Lau, W.S., Low, E., Seet, G.L. and Chin, C.S. (2009), A novel method to determine the hydrodynamic coefficients of an Eyeball ROV, *AIP Conference Proceedings*, 1089, pp. 11–22. doi: 10.1063/1.3078117.
56. Chin, C.S., Lau, M.W.S., Low, E. and Seet, G.G.L. (2006), A Cascaded Nonlinear Heading Control with Thrust Allocation: An Application on an Underactuated ROV, IEEE International Conferences on Robotics, Automation and Mechatronic (RAM), Bangkok, Thailand.
57. Chin, C.S., Lau, M.W.S., Low, E. and Seet, G.G.L. (2006), Design of Thrusters Configuration and Thrust Allocation Control for a Remotely Operated Vehicle, IEEE International Conferences on Robotics, Automation and Mechatronic (RAM), Bangkok, Thailand.
58. Chin, C.S., Lau, M.W.S., Low, E. and Seet, G.G.L. (2005), Analysis and Linear Control of a Low-Speed Maneuvering Underwater Robotic Vehicle (URV), 4th Asian Conference on Industrial Automation and Robotics, Bangkok, Thailand.
59. Chin, C.S. and Lau, M.W.S. (1999), Measurement and Control of a Thruster for Unmanned Robotic Vehicle (URV), 5th National Undergraduate Research Opportunities Programme (NUROP) Congress, NTU, Singapore.

# 2

## Development of ROV's Pilot Training Platform Using Unity™

### 2.1 Proposed Methodology Using Unity™

In this proposed methodology, the virtual simulation is to create a search operation on the subsea pipeline. A scenario will be set up where there will be a leakage in one of the jumpers and the task of the remotely operated vehicle (ROV) is to search for the location of the leakage and shut down that subsea system. The training simulation will be developed using the low-cost and off-the-shelf development tool.

Trainees will control the ROV model through a set of control systems consisting of a joystick, keyboard buttons, and graphical user interface (GUI) buttons, where the control system will transform the input received from the trainee into the virtual simulation. Trainees will have an interaction with the simulation through a GUI that will be displayed on the front panel. The current depth rating of the vehicle, time taken for the search operation, control panel for the activation of manipulators, and view of the ROV's position will be displayed on the front panel.

During the simulation, the ROV's position will be recorded at every frame in a regular time interval added into an array. It will then be exported into a text file at the end of the simulation. The trainees can review on their performance through the data collected and the recorded video of the simulation. The structure of the training simulation is shown in Figure 2.1.

### 2.2 Overall Software Structure

The hierarchy structure is shown in Figure 2.2. It briefly describes the overall simulation system. The system consists of four main elements: control input from a user, ROV control, data logging, and virtual scene.

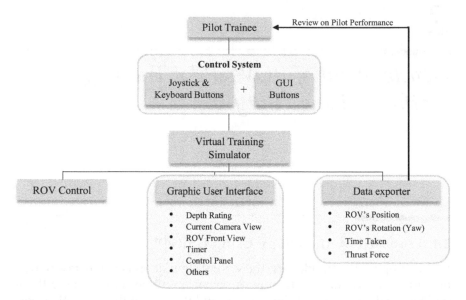

**FIGURE 2.1**
Structure of training simulator.

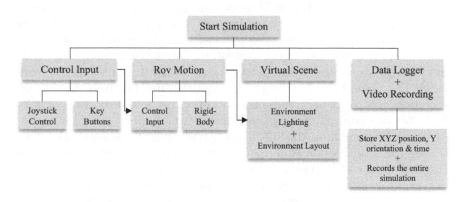

**FIGURE 2.2**
Simplified structure of the overall training simulation.

The control input system works in such a way that when it receives an input signal from the joystick or keyboard buttons, the system translates the signal into the virtual world. However, these signals do not directly affect the coordinate system of the ROV, nor does it affect the motion of the ROV. These signals have to be first applied to Unity's physics engine, rigidbody. The rigidbody component governs the ROV's motion according to the signal it receives. It controls the physical behavior of the ROV based on the different external forces that are applied to it.

At each time frame during the simulation, the data logger will store the ROV's position and orientation. These data are then exported in a text file, where trainees can view on their performance and the entire simulation through the recorded video. The virtual scene consists of integrating different 3D models to represent the subsea system, ParticleSystem for the underwater particles, and environment lighting. Unity's Global Illumination (GI) was used for environment lighting. The GI has great features that provide lighting-related settings and properties. Adjustments were made to compose the virtual environment.

## 2.3  Unity's Configurations and Setups

Unity3D is a flexible and powerful multiplatform that allows the designer to develop 2D and 3D games with an interactive experience. Designers can create a scene using C#, Java, or Boo script without complex coding that gives a great benefit for those who do not have the required programming skills. One unique feature of Unity3D is that 3D models can simply import as game assets into the software.

## 2.4  Unity™ Editor Interface

The Unity™ Editor interface (see Figure 2.3) shows the development of the project. It is important to familiarize with Unity™ Editor interface before developing a project. The essential functions required will be presented. The details of the interface can be seen in the website link: https://docs.unity3d.com/550/Documentation/Manual/UnityManual.html.

The default interface is tabbed with five windows: Scene View, toolbar, hierarchy, Inspector, and project window. Details of each window can be described as follows:

- **Scene View** – allows visual navigation and edit of scenes in 3D or 2D perspective depending on the type of project.
- **Toolbar** – provides access to the essential working features. On the left, it contains the basic tools for manipulating the Scene View and the objects within it. In the center are the play, pause, and step controls. The button to the right gives access to the Unity™

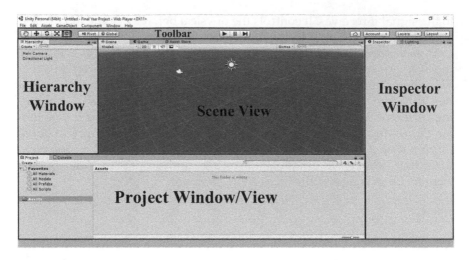

**FIGURE 2.3**
Unity™ Editor interface.

Cloud Services and Unity™ Account, followed by a layer visibility menu and finally the Editor layout menu that allows some alternate layouts for the Editor window.

- **Hierarchy Window** – represents every object in the scene. Each item in the scene has an entry in the hierarchy. The hierarchy shows the structure of how GameObjects are attached.
- **Inspector Window** – allows viewing and editing of all the properties of the current selected GameObject. As different types of GameObjects consist of different sets of properties/components, the layout and contents of the Inspector window can vary.
- **Project Window** – displays the library of assets that are available for the project. The game assets can be imported into Unity™ that appears in the project window.

The Scene View has navigation to allow users to move the object around

quickly and efficiently. The Scene Gizmo ![gizmo] is in the upper-right corner of the Scene View. This displays the Scene View and allows you to change the projection mode and viewing angle. The Scene Gizmo has a conical arm labeled X, Y, and Z. Click on any of the conical axis arms to snap the Scene View Camera to the axis (e.g., top view, front view, and left view). You can also right-click the cube at the center to bring up a menu with a list of viewing angles.

You can also toggle **Perspective** on and off. This changes the projection mode of the Scene View between Isometric and Perspective. To do this,

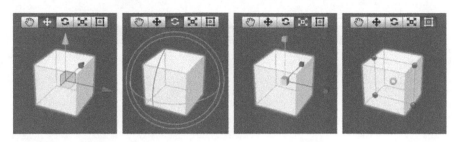

**FIGURE 2.4**
Transform tool.

click the cube in the center of the Scene Gizmo or the text below it. If your Scene View is in an awkward viewpoint that is quite confusing, Shift-click the cube at the center of the Scene Gizmo to return to Perspective view.

Alternatively, you can use the Arrow Keys to move around the Scene. The up and down arrows move the camera forward and backward in the direction it is facing. The left and right arrows pan the view sideways. Hold down the Shift key with an arrow to move faster. The Transform Tools used with the Scene View on the Toolbar can be used to move, rotate, and scale the GameObject as shown in Figure 2.4.

The Toolbar consists of other basic controls and relates to different parts of the Editor.

**Pivot** **Local** Transform Gizmo Toggles – affect the Scene View display

▶ ‖ ▶| Play/Pause/Step buttons – used with the Game View

☁ Cloud Button – opens the Unity™ Services Window

**Account** ▾ Account Drop-down – used to access your Unity™ Account

**Layers** ▾ Layers Drop-down – controls which objects are displayed in Scene View

**Layout** ▾ Layout Drop-down – controls the arrangement of all Views.

## 2.5 Installation of Unity™

To download and install Unity™ version 5.5.2, go to the unity website at https://unity3d.com/get-unity/download/archive. Unity™ provides two types of edition: personal edition and professional edition that requires

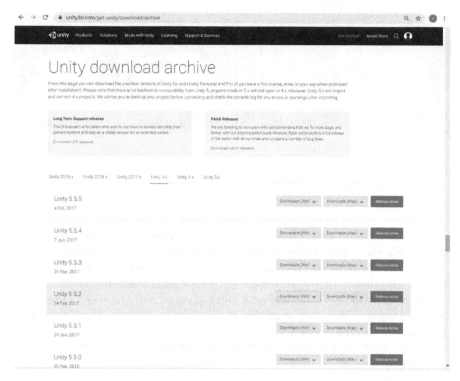

**FIGURE 2.5**
Main web page for downloading Unity™.

some costs. The personal edition will be downloaded to develop a simulator using low-cost software (see Figure 2.5).

Launch the download assistant, as shown in Figure 2.6, and click on next. Read the terms and conditions. Accept the terms of the license agreement, and click the Next button. Unity™ download assistant will provide a list of components in Figure 2.6. By default, the Unity 5.5.2f1, Documentation, Web Player, Standard Assets, Microsoft Visual Studio Tools for Unity™, and Windows Build Support will be selected, and click Next.

Next, specify the location to download and install the files. Set the location, as shown in Figure 2.7 and click on Next. Once the location is chosen, the download assistant will start to download the files. Wait until Unity™ has completed the download and installation. Now, the software is then ready for the project. The following sections provide a guide to developing the ROV Pilot Simulator.

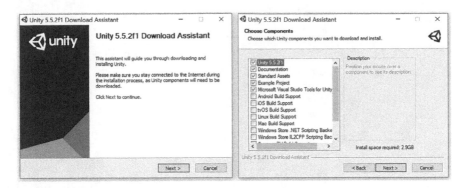

**FIGURE 2.6**
Download assistant and installation components.

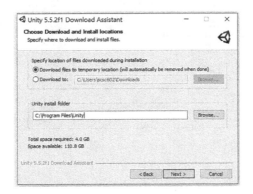

**FIGURE 2.7**
Choose download and install folder.

## 2.6 Create New Project

Open the Unity 5 Editor and select a new project on the top right-hand corner to create a new project. If a Unity™ project exists, the project will be shown in the home screen display as seen in Figure 2.8. Click the Project to launch the Unity™ Editor, or select Open to load existing project.

The home screen display will change to create a project view, as seen in Figure 2.9. There is an option to select Asset packages, as seen in Figure 2.9. It comes as a bundle with the Unity™ software. The Asset packages are selected by choosing the Asset packages and the preferred packages, or they can be imported later. In this case, none of the Asset packages were selected at the beginning.

**FIGURE 2.8**
Unity 5 home screen display.

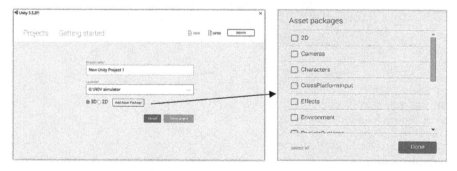

**FIGURE 2.9**
Create project view with asset packages option.

## 2.7 Developing Virtual Environment

One of the objectives is to create a virtual simulation of an ROV during a subsea pipeline inspection. A typical layout of a subsea production system can be seen as follows:

- Manifold
- Subsea X'mas tree

- Subsea
- Pipeline end terminations (PLET)
- Jumpers
- Pipelines.

The underwater scene consists of a subsea production system on the seabed, shown in Figure 2.10. The development of the virtual environment is broken down into four parts: creating the virtual seabed, importing of the subsea production system, creating underwater lighting, and creating underwater particles.

### 2.7.1 Virtual Seabed

The seabed of the virtual environment was created using a GameObject provided in Unity3D package called Terrain. The process of developing a virtual seabed is shown in Figure 2.11.

The first step is to set up a virtual environment. The virtual environment represents the underwater environment via a GameObject called Terrain. To create a Terrain, go to GameObject on the menu bar at the top left-hand corner, select 3D object and Terrain [GameObject → 3D Object → Terrain] as seen in Figure 2.12.

The Terrain will appear in the Scene View as a large flat plane. It will be added to the hierarchy window, as seen in Figure 2.13. Under the Inspector window, there are a few components attached to the GameObject: Transform, Terrain, and Terrain Collider.

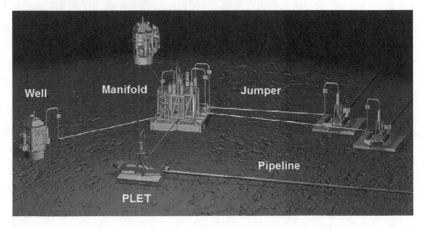

**FIGURE 2.10**
Typical layout of subsea production system.

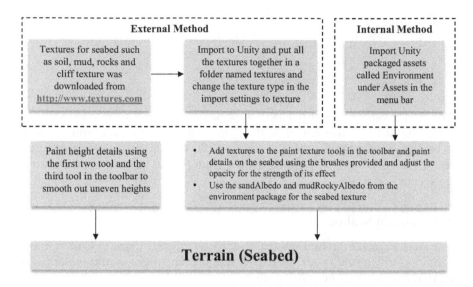

| External Method | | Internal Method |
|---|---|---|
| Textures for seabed such as soil, mud, rocks and cliff texture was downloaded from http://www.textures.com | Import to Unity and put all the textures together in a folder named textures and change the texture type in the import settings to texture | Import Unity packaged assets called Environment under Assets in the menu bar |

Paint height details using the first two tool and the third tool in the toolbar to smooth out uneven heights

- Add textures to the paint texture tools in the toolbar and paint details on the seabed using the brushes provided and adjust the opacity for the strength of its effect
- Use the sandAlbedo and mudRockyAlbedo from the environment package for the seabed texture

**Terrain (Seabed)**

**FIGURE 2.11**
Process of developing virtual seabed.

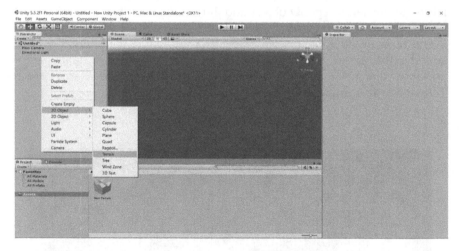

**FIGURE 2.12**
Set up Terrain.

- **Transform** – The transform component is the most common component attached to the GameObject where it can be used to set the position, rotation, and the scale of the object in the X, Y, and Z-Axes
- **Terrain** – The Terrain component provides a toolbar for several useful tools for different environment features

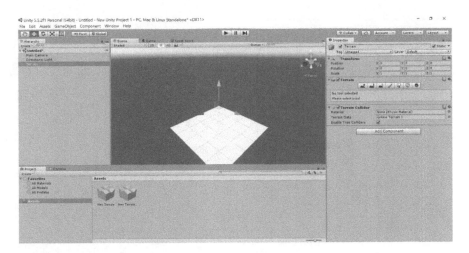

**FIGURE 2.13**
Scene View with Terrain added with axis at center.

- **Terrain Collider** – The Terrain Collider component generates a collision surface with the same shape as the Terrain object

To make the flat plain Terrain into a seabed, use the tools in the Terrain toolbar provided, as shown in Figure 2.14. The first three tools are used to change the height of the Terrain. It comes with a different set of brushes and settings (brush size and opacity). The size simply means adjusting the brush size and the strength of the brushes.

Before painting the height of the Terrain, go to the setting tools (the last tool on the Terrain toolbar) and under resolution set the Terrain width, length, and height to 2000, 2000, and 850, respectively (see Figure 2.15) and set its transform position to –1000, –800, and –1000 (see Figure 2.16), respectively. By setting the transform to –1000 on the X- and Z-Axes,

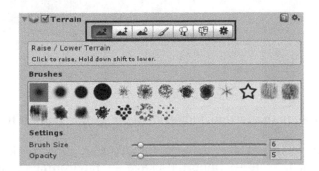

**FIGURE 2.14**
Terrain component in Inspector window.

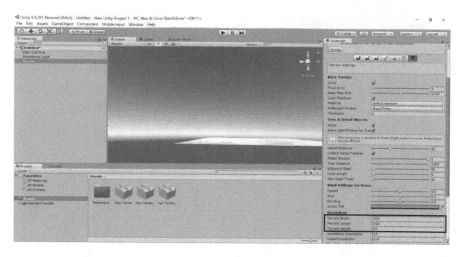

**FIGURE 2.15**
Set Terrain width, length, and height of seabed.

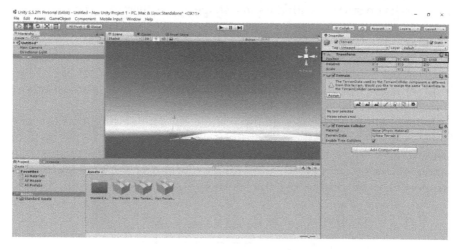

**FIGURE 2.16**
Set transform position of seabed.

it will centralize the Terrain and −800 on the Y-Axis will set the depth of the seabed.

To have more texture variety, import the asset package called Environment [Assets → Import Package → Environment], as seen in Figure 2.17. The environment package has a variety of texture; the sandAlbedo and mudRockyAlbedo will be used to give the seabed some details.

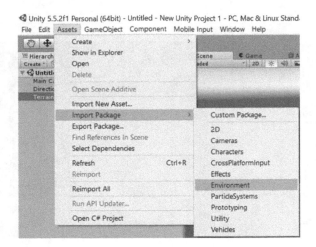

**FIGURE 2.17**
Import the asset package called Environment.

After importing the environment package (it will take a few minutes), click on edit textures, and add textures. Select the sandAlbedo and mudRockyAlbedo from the option as seen in Figure 2.18. Ensure that the sandAlbedo is selected first as it forms the base texture of the Terrain. Next, use the mudRockyAlbedo to paint some details on the Terrain such that it looks like a seabed.

Alternatively, additional texture images can be obtained from **http://www.textures.com/** as seen in Figure 2.19. An online website provides a wide variety of texture images ranging from soil, rocks, metal, rust, and other textures. An example of how to download textures from the website and import it into Unity™ to use it as a paint texture will be explained.

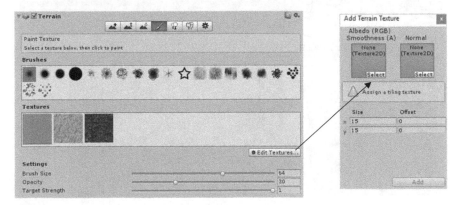

**FIGURE 2.18**
Terrain paint texture and add Terrain texture.

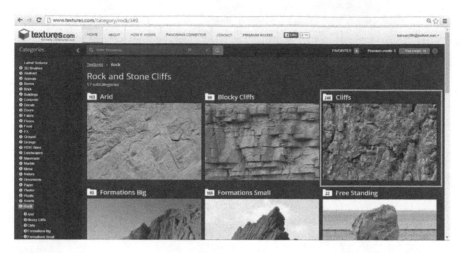

**FIGURE 2.19**
Texture website.

As seen in Figure 2.20, there is an underwater cliff created on the Terrain using the height tools. To make it more realistic and have a cliffy look, download a texture image called cliffs0193 from https://www.textures.com/search?q=Cliffs0193 [Rock → Cliffs → Cliffs0193].

Next, download the small (1024×1024) texture image as shown in Figure 2.21, and save it in the desktop. Import the texture as a new asset in the project window. To import the texture into the Editor interface, go to the asset in the menu bar and select import new assets [Assets → Import

**FIGURE 2.20**
Cliffs0193 texture image.

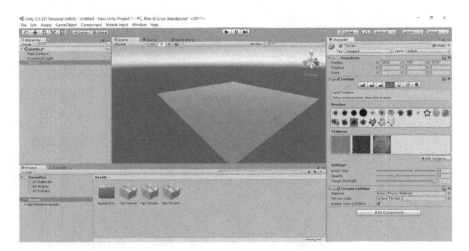

**FIGURE 2.21**
Texture of Terrain.

New Asset]. To start painting the details of the underwater cliff, go to the painting tool in the Terrain component, select Edit, and Add texture. Ensure that the cliff texture is selected in the texture property. Select the appropriate brush, and paint the underwater cliff. As seen in Figure 2.21, the Terrain is no longer a white plane.

The first three tools from the left in the toolbar are the height tools. The first tool is the Raise/Lower Terrain, where it is used to increase/decrease the height of the Terrain and the height will accumulate if the mouse is held in place. To increase the height of the Terrain, click on any position on the Terrain with the mouse. To decrease the height, hold down the Shift key and click. The user can flatten the Terrain or move the base of the Terrain higher in Figure 2.22.

The second tool from the left is the paint height. It is similar to the first tool with an additional property to set target height. The third tool is the Smooth Height different from the first two tools, where it is used to smooth out any edges or average out the painted height. The seabed is shown in Figure 2.23. Rename the Terrain by right-clicking on the Terrain in the hierarchy and select rename the Seabed.

Lastly, save the scene as rov_scene as shown in Figure 2.24.

## 2.7.2 Importing of Subsea 3D Models

Three-dimensional models will be imported into the Assets folder, as shown in Figure 2.25. It has a set of Import Settings not only for the 3D models but also available for each asset. The 3D models of subsea production systems consist of the manifold, PLET, subsea tree, jumpers, and pipeline

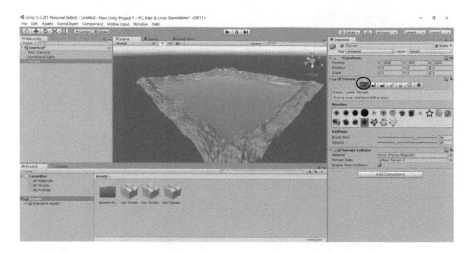

**FIGURE 2.22**
Use of height tool for Terrain.

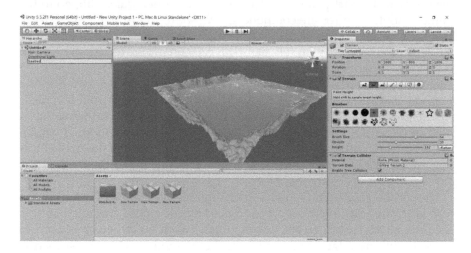

**FIGURE 2.23**
Rename Terrain as Seabed.

downloaded from SketchUp 3D Warehouse or https://3dwarehouse.
sketchup.com/search/?q=subsea. Each model was exported out from
SketchUp in ".fbx" file format such that it can be imported into Unity3D.
It is vital to ensure that the file format is compatible and readable in
Unity3D. For example, file formats such as ".obj", ".ma", ".fbx", and ".dae"
are accepted.

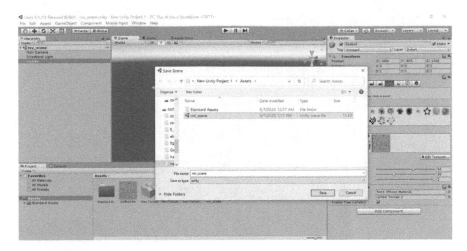

**FIGURE 2.24**
Save scene as rov_scene.

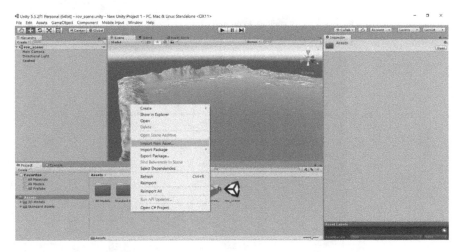

**FIGURE 2.25**
Import 3D models into Assets.

Then, select the TRV-M ROV model as shown: Assets→3D Models→→ TRV-M ROV in Figure 2.26.

The options displayed on the import setting vary for TRV-M ROV (see Figure 2.27). The import settings can be modified to change the appearance such as the scale factor and the behavior of the asset. To view and make changes in the import settings, select on TRV-M ROV model from the project window. The import settings in the Inspector window are shown in Figure 2.27. The first setting to change is the scale factor.

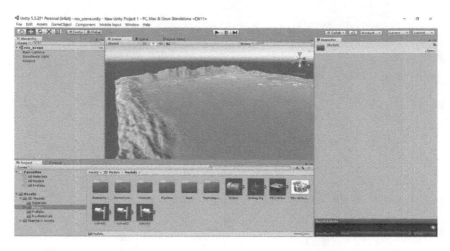

**FIGURE 2.26**
Open 3D model such as TRV-M ROV (http://ssirovs.com/wp-content/uploads/2018/02/TRV-M_Specs.pdf).

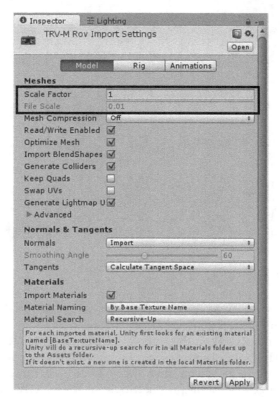

**FIGURE 2.27**
TRV-M ROV import settings.

The ROV model has been imported into Unity™, which has a default file scale of 0.01 units. It implies that the 3D model fbx file is imported into Unity™; the model file has been scaled down to a default scaling of 0.01 units instead of its original scale. If the ROV model is added into the scene window, it will look extremely small. To compensate for the difference in the units between Unity™ and the external 3D model file, change the scale factor in the import settings. Note that 1 unit in Unity's Physics Engine is equivalent to 1 m. For the ROV model, its scale factor was changed to 100 to gain its original scale dimension.

Drag the "TRV-M ROV model" in Project View into the Scene View, as seen in Figure 2.28. In the Hierarchy Window, click "TRV-M ROV" and double-click on "TRV_M__Submersible_Systems1".

The next setting is to adjust the generate colliders, where it will create a collision mesh to allow the model to collide with other objects. It is only useful for making a collision mesh for environment geometry. Since the ROV model is maneuvering around the scene via external control, uncheck the box next to the generate collider property. The colliders for ROV can be created (see Figures 2.29 and 2.30).

After these two adjustments have been made, click to apply these changes. The scale factor needs to change for the remaining 3D models.

- Manifold
- PLET
- Jumper
- X'mas Tree

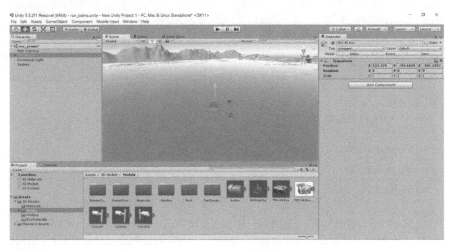

**FIGURE 2.28**
TRV-M ROV in Scene View.

**FIGURE 2.29**
Add component such as box collider in Inspector View.

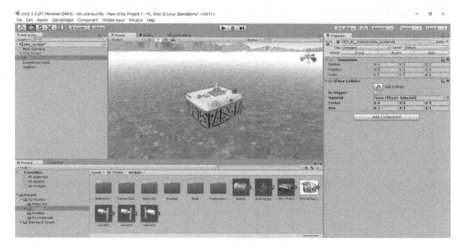

**FIGURE 2.30**
Box collider for TRV-M-ROV.

- Pipeline (straight pipes)
- Pipe Bent
- Valves.

The generate collider box for the 3D models is set accordingly in Table 2.1.

The function of a collider is to create a collision mesh around the object such that it will collide with other objects in the scene in the real world. Since the ROV is a mobile object, it is advisable to use a box collider

**TABLE 2.1**

Import Settings for Different 3D Models

| 3D Model | Scale Factor | Generate Colliders |
|---|---|---|
| TRV-M ROV | 400 | Unchecked |
| Manifold | 100 | Checked |
| PLET | 100 | Checked |
| Jumper | 100 | Checked |
| X'mas Tree | 100 | Checked |
| Pipeline (straight pipes) | 100 | Checked |
| Pipe Bent | 100 | Checked |
| Valves | 100 | Checked |

instead of generating the colliders in the import setting. The colliders can be added through the add component tab in the Inspector window under the physics section. The configuration for the jaw colliders was set when the manipulators are not used during the simulation. The colliders for the jaws will be deactivated. It prevents the jaw collider from colliding with the main collider around the ROV model as it can affect the result data.

The next step is to construct the layout of the subsea production, as shown in Figure 2.31. The models were arranged and linked together using the jumpers and pipeline to form the layout of the subsea production system. The entire schematic layout is categorized into three sections:

- Top section
- Bottom section
- Center section.

The final subsea production system is shown in Figure 2.32.

To add the 3D models into the Scene View, drag and drop the model into the Scene View. The model will appear on the Scene View and the hierarchy window as seen in Figure 2.33.

The current position of the center manifold can be seen under the transform component located in the Inspector window. As the whole subsea oil layout was constructed in SketchUp and exported about the global axis, the transform position of all the 3D models is set to (0, 0, 0). As can be seen from Figure 2.34, all 3D models are connected with the transform position set to (0, 0, 0). A similar approach is performed for the Top Section, as seen in Figure 2.35. Figure 2.36 shows the entire process of importing the 3D models into the Scene View.

The subsea models are set as a child of the _Subsea System. If the position of the models needs to be modified, it will be performed under the parent transform component instead of changing all individual models

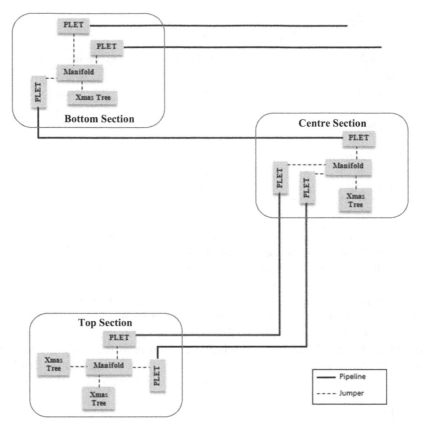

**FIGURE 2.31**
Arrangement of subsea production system.

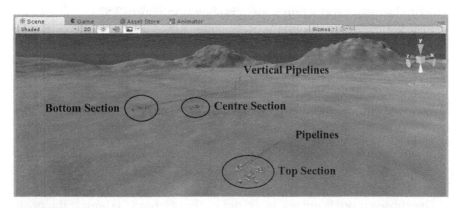

**FIGURE 2.32**
Subsea production layout.

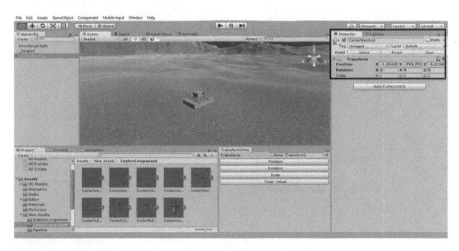

**FIGURE 2.33**
Adding model to Scene View.

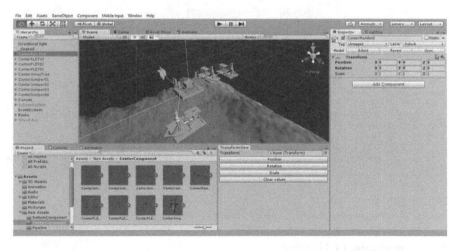

**FIGURE 2.34**
Centre section of subsea layout.

in the scene. In Unity3D, the world space coordinates are set in a way that the X- and Z-Axes represent coordinates in the horizontal direction. The Y-Axis represents the vertical direction. Rotation around the X-Axis gives a pitching motion ($\theta$); rotation around the Z-Axis generates a rolling motion ($\varphi$). On the other hand, rotation around the Y-Axis produces a yawing motion ($\psi$) (Figure 2.37).

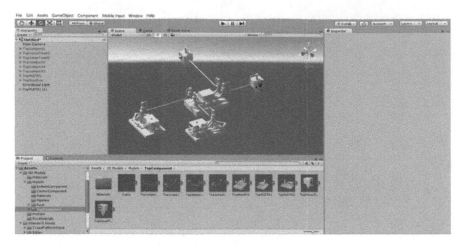

**FIGURE 2.35**
Top section of subsea layout.

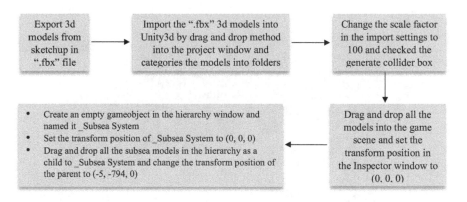

**FIGURE 2.36**
Process of importing and creating virtual subsea system.

### 2.7.3 Environment Lighting

As most of the ROV search operations are performed in deep waters, there is very little light penetrating through it. The virtual simulation needs to provide an accurate representation of the environment to its end-user. An increase in the amount of fidelity will have an impact on the performance during the operation.

The environment lighting can be set by using a directional light, which is an asset that is provided by Unity3D. Directional light is a large, distant source that comes from a position outside the range of the virtual world. In other words, the directional light can be represented as the sun or the moon.

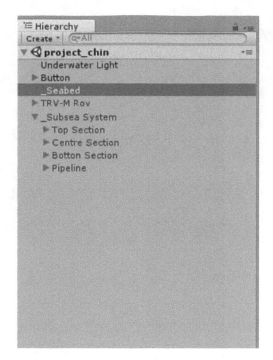

**FIGURE 2.37**
Set all subsea models as _Subsea System.

Figure 2.38 shows the process of creating a directional light and its parameters. The underwater lighting is shown in Figure 2.39.

The lighting window in Unity3D [Menu: Window → Lighting] is the main control point for Unity's GI features. It contains lighting-related settings and properties that allow the user to modify many aspects of the GI process. The two settings that can be adjusted in the lighting window to recreate the underwater environment are as follows:

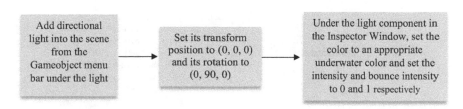

**FIGURE 2.38**
Creating directional light.

**FIGURE 2.39**
Unity's directional light settings.

- Environment lighting [Menu: Window → Lighting → environment lighting]
- Fog [Menu: Window → Lighting → fog].

The steps taken to create an underwater environment are shown in Figure 2.40.

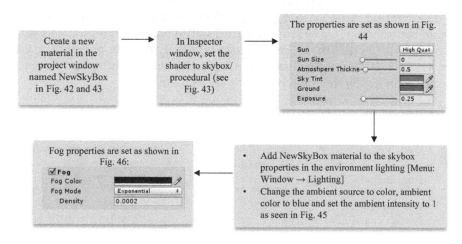

**FIGURE 2.40**
Flow diagram of developing underwater environment.

Create a new material in the project window named NewSkyBox, which is shown in in Figures 2.41 and 2.42.

The properties are set in Figures 2.43–2.45, where the underwater color becomes quite prominent.

**FIGURE 2.41**
Create new material in project window named NewSkyBox.

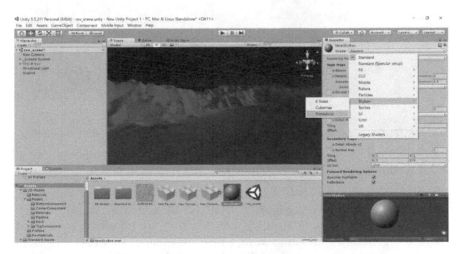

**FIGURE 2.42**
Create new material in project window named NewSkyBox.

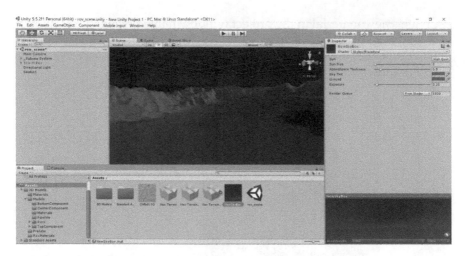

**FIGURE 2.43**
Properties settings for NewSkyBox.

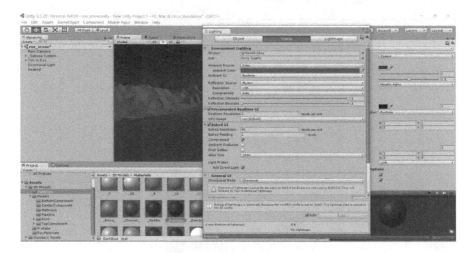

**FIGURE 2.44**
Add NewSkyBox material to the skybox properties in lighting [Menu: Window → Lighting].

## 2.7.4 Underwater Particles

The ParticleSystem in Unity3D is used to create the underwater particle. The ParticleSystem is a component that can be added as a child to any GameObject. It can simulate fluid entities such as liquids, clouds, and flames by generating and animating a large number of small 2D images in the scene. Particles consist of small and straightforward images or meshes that are displayed and moved in high quantities by a ParticleSystem.

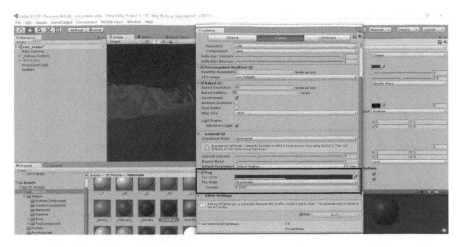

**FIGURE 2.45**
Add Fog in lighting [Menu: Window → Lighting].

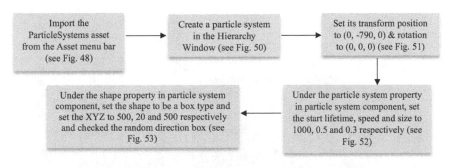

**FIGURE 2.46**
Steps in developing underwater particles.

There are several properties in the ParticleSystem that can be adjusted. Figure 2.46 shows the steps in creating the underwater particle using the ParticleSystem, while Figure 2.47 shows the virtual environment with underwater particles being added to the scene.

It takes around a few seconds to import the ParticleSystems into the Project Window under the Standard Assets folder. As seen in Figure 2.48, click import to complete the process.

Then create a ParticleSystem in the Hierarchy Window in Figure 2.49.

Set its transform position to (0, –790, 0) and rotation to (0, 0, 0) as seen in Inspector View in Figure 2.50.

Under the ParticleSystem property in the ParticleSystem component, set the start lifetime, speed, and size to 1000, 0.5, and 0.3, respectively (see Figure 2.51).

**FIGURE 2.47**
Import ParticleSystems asset from Asset menu bar.

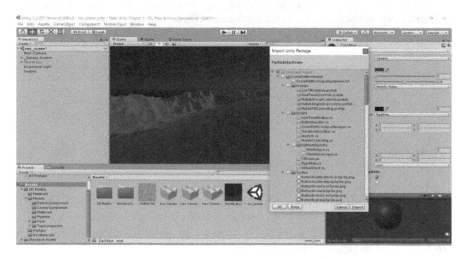

**FIGURE 2.48**
Import ParticleSystems asset from Asset menu bar in few seconds.

As shown in Figure 2.52, under the shape property in the ParticleSystem component, set the shape to be a box type and XYZ to 500, 20, and 500, respectively, and check the random direction box. The completed underwater particle is shown in Figure 2.53.

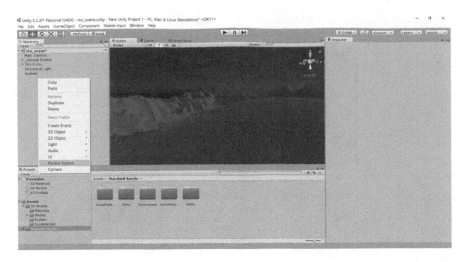

**FIGURE 2.49**
Create ParticleSystem in Hierarchy Window.

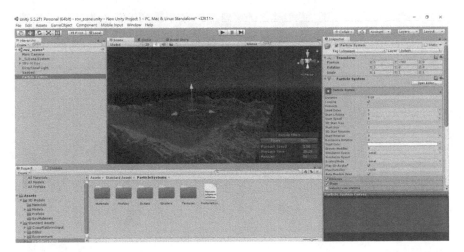

**FIGURE 2.50**
Set its transform position and rotation for ParticleSystems.

## 2.8 ROV Model and Specification

Since the ROV is used to inspect the subsea pipeline, the key criteria in selecting the ROV model are its depth rating. In this book, the "TRV-M" ROV constructed by Submersible Systems Inc. was chosen. Although

**FIGURE 2.51**
Set start lifetime, speed, and size for ParticleSystem components.

**FIGURE 2.52**
Set shape for ParticleSystem components.

several types of ROVs can satisfy the same working depth, the 3D models were not available in SketchUp. Therefore, the "TRV-M" was selected as a simulation model. The actual model of the TRV-M ROV is shown in Figure 2.54, while the simulation model of the TRV-M ROV is shown in Figure 2.54. Refer to Appendix A for TRV-M ROV technical specification or the link: http://ssirovs.com/wp-content/uploads/2018/02/TRV-M_Specs.pdf.

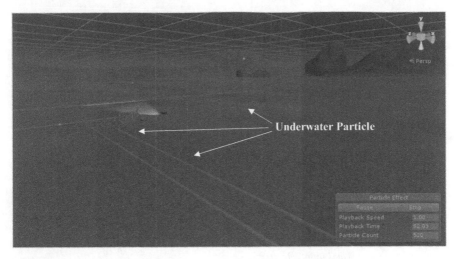

**FIGURE 2.53**
Virtual environment with underwater particles.

**FIGURE 2.54**
TRV-M ROV actual and simulation model.

The TRV-M ROV is coupled with five thrusters (port, starboard, lateral, and two vertical) that allow the model to perform at 4kt forward, 3kt aft, and 3kt lateral. The underwater vehicle can maneuver forward, reverse, lateral, and vertical, and rotate at a speed of 120°/s. The basic properties of the TRV-M ROV are shown in Table 2.2.

## 2.9 Configuration of TRV-M in Virtual Simulation

A typical underwater vehicle consists of six degrees of freedom (DOF) in motion. The vehicle can move in the surge, sway and heave and pitch, yaw, and roll for the ROV's orientation. However, in this simulation, surge,

**TABLE 2.2**

Properties of TRV-M ROV

| Properties | Values | |
|---|---|---|
| *General Specification* | | |
| Depth rating | 1000 | m |
| Height | 610 | mm |
| Length | 1524 | mm |
| Width | 48 | mm |
| Weight in air | 426.37 | kg |
| *Maximum Static Thrust* | | |
| Forward | 230 | lbs |
| Reverse | 150 | lbs |
| Lateral | 110 | lbs |
| Vertical | 230 | lbs |
| *Maximum Velocity* | | |
| Forward | 2.04 | m/s |
| Reverse | 1.53 | m/s |
| Lateral | 1.02 | m/s |
| Vertical | 3 | m/s |
| Turning rate | 120 | °/s |

sway, heave, and yaw motion are allowed for ROV. Figure 2.55 shows the DOF of the ROV. Note that Unity3D has its world coordinate set differently.

Therefore, the surge motion of the ROV will be in the Z-Axis, while the sway motion will be in the X-Axis, the heave motion will be in the Y-Axis, and lastly, the yaw motion will be rotated around the Y-Axis. A forward movement in the Z-Axis will produce a positive surge value, the right

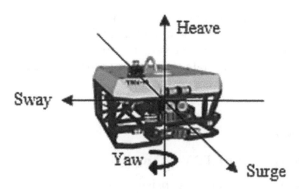

**FIGURE 2.55**

TRV-M four degree of freedom in virtual world.

move in the X-Axis will give a positive sway value, and finally, rotation in the clockwise direction will deliver a positive yaw value.

The ROV model was obtained from SketchUp and exported in ".fbx" file format for importation into Unity3D. Similar to the subsea models, the scale factor of the ROV is changed to 100 units. Since the ROV is a mobile GameObject, the colliders will not be generated in the import settings.

A rigidbody component is added to the ROV model in the simulation. The rigidbody component can be attached through the add component tab in the Inspector window under the physics category. Different configurations were made to the properties in the rigidbody component as seen in Figure 2.56. Refer to Appendix B for the function of each property. The ROV mass is set according to its original mass that is 426.37 kg, and the rigidbody will experience drag and angular drag force that is set to 1 and 0.05, respectively. The body is constrained on the X rotation and Z rotation. It will not cause the underwater vehicle to rotate around the X- or Z-Axis.

As there were no colliders generated in the import settings, three primitive box colliders are added to the ROV in Figure 2.56. Similar to the rigidbody component, the colliders can be added through the add component tab in the Inspector window under the physics section. Two colliders were placed around the manipulator jaw, as shown in Figure 2.57. The settings for all three box colliders are shown in Table 2.3. The completed model with box colliders is shown in Figure 2.58.

Another component that was added to the ROV model was the camera component. It captures and displays the world to the player. Different settings can be made to the properties of the cameras. There are four cameras

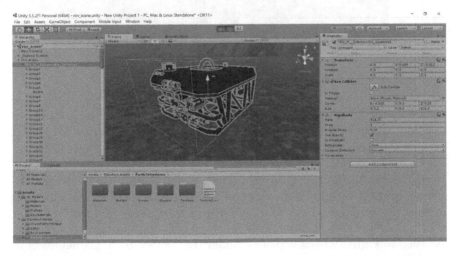

**FIGURE 2.56**
Rigidbody and box collider components added to TRV-M ROV model.

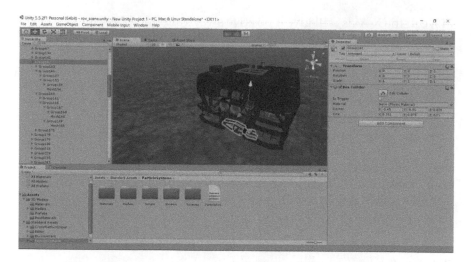

**FIGURE 2.57**
Box collider component added to manipulator jaw.

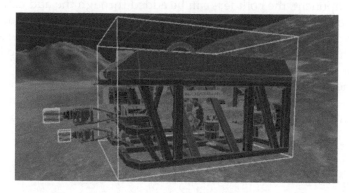

**FIGURE 2.58**
Side view of ROV with box colliders attached.

added as a child to the ROV GameObject, and the settings for each camera are tabulated in Table 2.4. For example, the primary camera is shown in Figure 2.59. The completed cameras settings are shown in Figure 2.60.

The next component that is added to the ROV model is the light component. Since there is very little light in the virtual environment, the end-user can use this light component on the ROV to assist the maneuvering around the virtual world. The light component is set to be a Spotlight that has a specified location and range that is constrained to an angle. As seen in Figure 2.61, it is placed under the TRV-M ROV GameObject in the Hierarchy View. The settings for the light component are tabulated in Table 2.5. The completed settings for the Spotlight are shown in Figure 2.62.

**TABLE 2.3**

Properties for ROV Collider

| Item/Properties | | ROV Body | Left Jaw | Right Jaw |
|---|---|---|---|---|
| Enabled | | Yes | No | No |
| Is Trigger | | No | No | No |
| Material | | None | None | None |
| **Center** | X | −0.025 | 0.5 | −0.45 |
| | Y | 0.3 | −0.01 | −0.01 |
| | Z | 0.15 | 0.005 | 0.025 |
| **Size** | X | 1.2 | 0.151 | 0.151 |
| | Y | 0.9 | 0.075 | 0.075 |
| | Z | 1.6 | 0.11 | 0.11 |

**TABLE 2.4**

Properties for Camera Settings

| Camera Name/ Properties | Main Camera | Back Camera | Third-Person View | Front View |
|---|---|---|---|---|
| Clear flags | Skybox | Skybox | Skybox | Skybox |
| Background | ▬▬▬ | ▬▬▬ | ▬▬▬ | ▬▬▬ |
| Culling mask | Everything | Everything | Everything | Everything |
| Projection | Perspective | Perspective | Perspective | Perspective |
| Field of view | 60 | 60 | 40 | 30 |
| Clipping planes (near/far) | 0.05/1000 | 0.05/1000 | 0.3/1000 | 0.3/1000 |
| **Viewport** X | 0 | 0 | 0 | 0.79 |
| **Rect** Y | 0 | 0 | 0 | 0.73 |
| W | 1 | 1 | 1 | 0.2 |
| H | 1 | 1 | 1 | 0.25 |
| Depth | 0 | 0 | 0 | 1 |
| Rendering path | Use player settings | Use player settings | Use player settings | Use player settings |
| Target texture | None | None | None | None |
| Occlusion culling | Checked | Checked | Checked | Checked |
| HDR | Unchecked | Unchecked | Unchecked | Unchecked |

The last configuration was creating animation clips for the propellers and its manipulators. Unity3D provides a sophisticated and rich animation system that allows easy workflow and setups for all elements in Unity™. The animation system can be used to animate the following:

- Rotation of the propellers
- Activation of the manipulators.

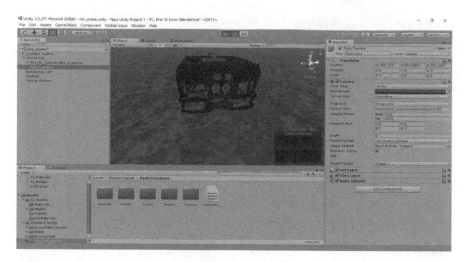

**FIGURE 2.59**
Main camera settings for ROV.

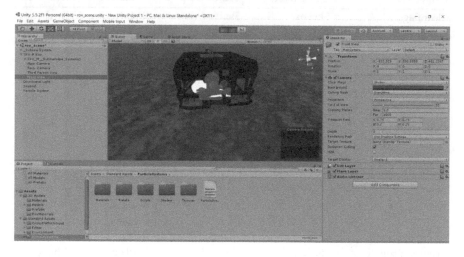

**FIGURE 2.60**
Other cameras settings for ROV.

The animation clips are created through an extra tab called animation in Figure 2.63. Click "Create", and save the animation, as shown in Figure 2.64.

To create the animation clips, the property of the object that requires animation has to be added. Figure 2.65 shows how to add the property of CentreBlades in animation.

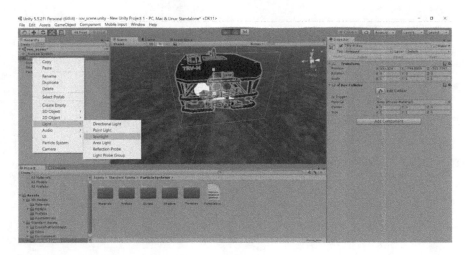

**FIGURE 2.61**
Spotlight GameObject for ROV.

**TABLE 2.5**

Properties for the Light Component

| Properties | Configuration |
|---|---|
| Type | Spot |
| Baking | Realtime |
| Range | 80 |
| Spot angle | 30 |
| Color | |
| Intensity | 6 |
| Bounce intensity | 0 |
| Shadow type | Soft shadow |
| Strength | 1 |
| Resolution | Use quality settings |
| Bias | 0.05 |
| Normal bias | 0.4 |
| Near plane | 0.2 |
| Cookie | None |
| Draw halo | Unchecked |
| Flare | None |
| Render mode | Auto |
| Culling mask | Everything |

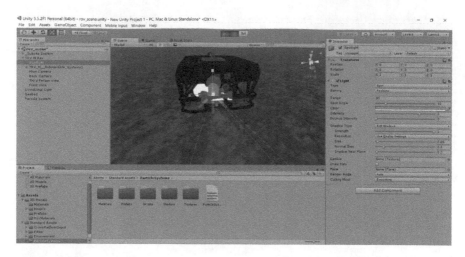

**FIGURE 2.62**
Spotlight settings for ROV.

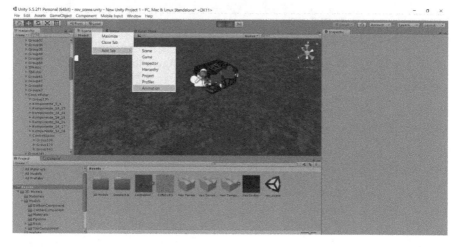

**FIGURE 2.63**
Create animation tab.

Figure 2.66 shows the first and second keys of the CentreBlades for animation.

As seen in Figure 2.67, the transform rotation of the center propeller is added so that rotation of the object can be changed at different keys. Since the center propeller is facing towards the X-Axis, the rotation of the propeller blades will be around the X-Axis. The first key is set to zero on the x rotation, and the second key is set to −720. It means that the propeller blades will rotate 720°/s. The same settings are set for the two rear

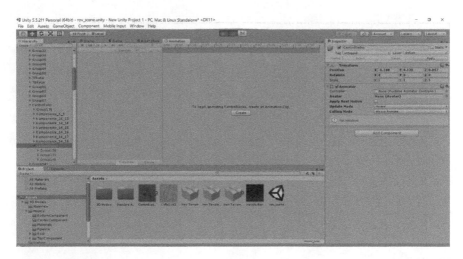

**FIGURE 2.64**
Create animation clip.

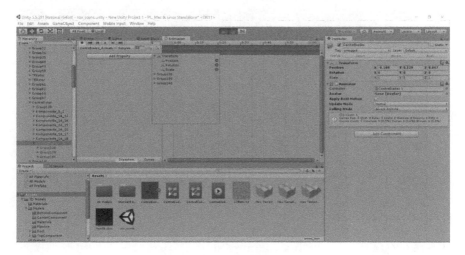

**FIGURE 2.65**
Add property in animation.

propellers (720°/s for right-back propeller and –720°/s for left-back propeller) and the top propellers (720°/s for both front and back top propellers).

For the top and back propellers, an additional animation clip was added in the animator window as seen in Figure 2.68 and a Boolean parameter is set to the animator controller. The "PropellerIdle" is just an empty animation clip; this is added as we do not want the back and top propeller to rotate during simulation until it receives an input from the user. It means that when the simulation starts, the entry state will make a transition to

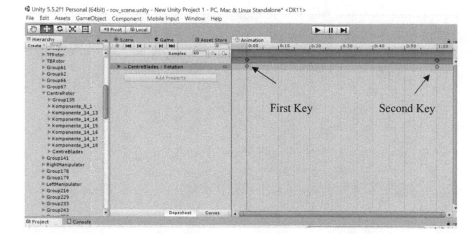

**FIGURE 2.66**
Animation window.

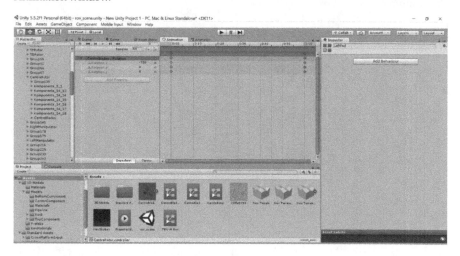

**FIGURE 2.67**
Animation window.

the idle state. If the parameter is set to false, the "LeftRotate" state will go back to the idle state. The different states can be seen as follows:

- Any state (see Figure 2.68)
- PropellerIdle (see Figure 2.69)
- Entry (see Figure 2.70)
- Left rotate (see Figure 2.71).

The final states for animation are shown in Figure 2.72. Click on LeftRotate-> PropellerIdle under Transitions to see the settings. The user

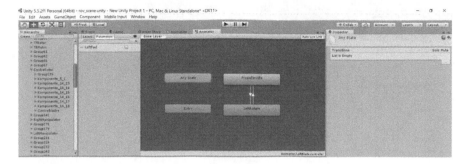

**FIGURE 2.68**
Any state used in animator.

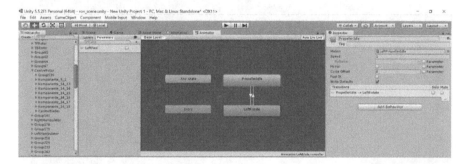

**FIGURE 2.69**
PropellerIdle state used in animator.

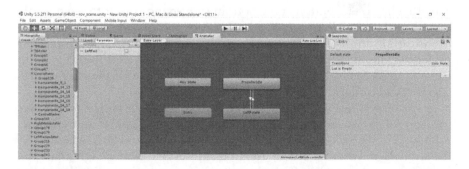

**FIGURE 2.70**
Entry state used in animator.

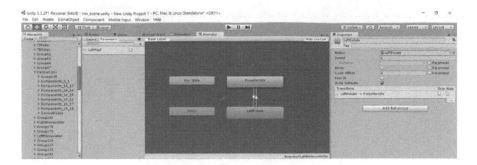

**FIGURE 2.71**
Left rotate state used in animator.

**FIGURE 2.72**
Settings in animator window.

can also click ▶ button at the bottom right-hand corner to see the animation of the propeller.

Ensure all animation files are saved in the folder named Animation under the Assets as seen in Figure 2.73. It allows the user to retrieve the files required easily. Note that the 3D model of the blades used in animation is saved under the same folder (see Figure 2.73).

The same settings were made for the ROV manipulators. The manipulators consist of two animation clips as seen in Figure 2.74: an idle clip and rotation clip. The rotation of the manipulators is around its Y-Axis and in the animation window, and the rotation clip for the left and right manipulators was set to negative 90 and position 90, respectively. Similar to the propeller, the idle animation is just an empty animation clip.

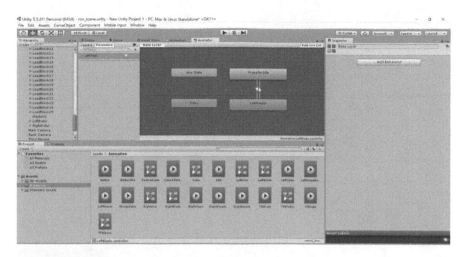

**FIGURE 2.73**
Animation files in folder named animation under Assets.

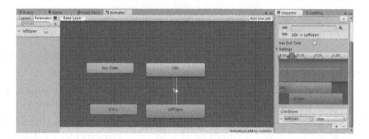

**FIGURE 2.74**
Manipulator settings in animator window.

A Boolean parameter was set for both manipulators – "leftOpen" and "rightOpen" – when it receives an input from the user. If it gets an opposite input from the user, it will set the parameter to false.

## 2.10  Controller Input

In the real world, the ROVs are controlled by pilots through a set of the vehicle control box made up of joysticks and buttons. The control system consists of a flight joystick (Logitech Extreme 3D Pro Joystick) and a keyboard. These two sets of controller devices are used to translate the movement received from the end-user into the virtual world. The development

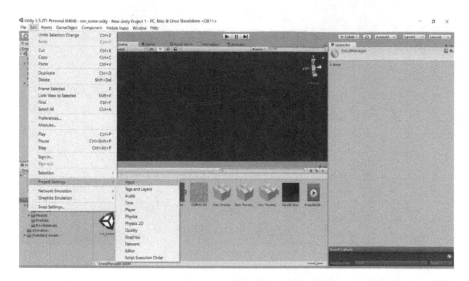

**FIGURE 2.75**
Open Input Manager.

of the control inputs is divided into three parts: ROV controller, manipulators controller, and the camera controller.

The three inputs are as follows: (1) X- and Z-Axes of the joystick. (2) The Y- and X-Axes of the joystick control the surge and sway motion while the Z-Axis controls the rotation about the Y-Axis (yaw) of the underwater vehicle. (3) The heave motion of the ROV is controlled by the 5th (up) and 6th (down) button on the joystick. These will be the control input for the translational and rotational motion of the ROV. To see the Input Manager, choose Edit->Project Settings->Input. See Figure 2.75 for the Input Manager.

The control inputs will be defined in the Input Manager as shown in Figure 2.76. The input settings for the horizontal axis are shown in Figure 2.77.

The manipulators of the ROV are controlled by a GUI button on the front panel. It allows users to activate and deactivate the manipulators at the touch of a button. The subsequent section will explain the use of a GUI system. The manipulators will be controlled by a few keys on the keyboard. These four key codes are defined in the input manager, which are given as follows:

- Keycode Q (left rotation) and E (right rotation) for the left jaw
- Keycode I (left rotation) and P (right rotation) for the right jaw.

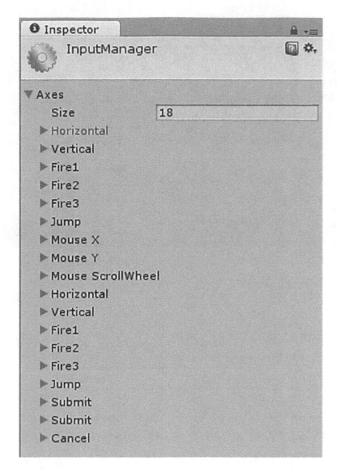

**FIGURE 2.76**
Input Manager.

The next input axes are the camera controller. There are four cameras in the scene; the main camera, back camera, a third-person view camera, and lastly, a camera projecting the front view of the underwater vehicle itself. The first three cameras are interchangeable using the joystick button 11, and the control button will be coded in the C# script. The panning and tilting of the main (and back camera) are controlled by the hat on the joystick.

Therefore, nine axes need to define in the input manager, and each input axes will have different properties to it. The name of each axis (see Table 2.6) and its properties settings are summarized in Table 2.7. Figure 2.78 shows the joystick axes and buttons. Refer to Appendix B for the function of each property. Note that the joystick needs to be properly installed, as shown in Appendix C.

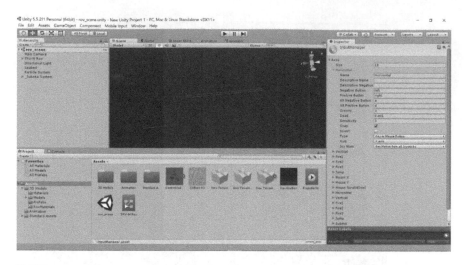

**FIGURE 2.77**
Horizontal axis in Input Manager.

**TABLE 2.6**

Control Inputs and Function

| Control Inputs | Functions |
| --- | --- |
| *ROV Controller* | |
| Joystick Y-Axis | Forward/Reverse movement |
| Joystick X-Axis | Lateral movement |
| Joystick 3rd axis | Yaw |
| Joystick throttle | Power control |
| Joystick buttons 5 & 6 | Vertical movement |
| *Camera Controller* | |
| Joystick POV Y-Axis | Tilt |
| Joystick POV X-Axis | Pan |
| Joystick button 11 | Switch camera view |
| *Light Controller* | |
| Joystick button 2 | Light switch |
| *Manipulators Controller* | |
| Keycode Q & E | Left jaw rotation |
| Keycode I & P | Right jaw rotation |
| GUI button | Activation of manipulators |

**TABLE 2.7**

Properties of ROV Control Input

| Function/ Properties | | | ROV Controller | | |
|---|---|---|---|---|---|
| Name | Joystick forward | Joystick lateral | Joystick button 5 & 6 | Joystick yaw | Throttle |
| Negative button | – | – | Joystick button 5 | – | – |
| Positive button | – | – | Joystick button 4 | – | – |
| Gravity | 0 | 0 | 1 | 0 | 0 |
| Dead | 0.19 | 0.19 | 0.001 | 0.05 | 0.19 |
| Sensitivity | 1 | 1 | 1 | 0.1 | 1 |
| Type | Joystick axis | Joystick axis | Key or mouse button | Joystick axis | Joystick axis |
| Axis | Y-Axis | X-Axis | – | 3rd axis | 4th axis |

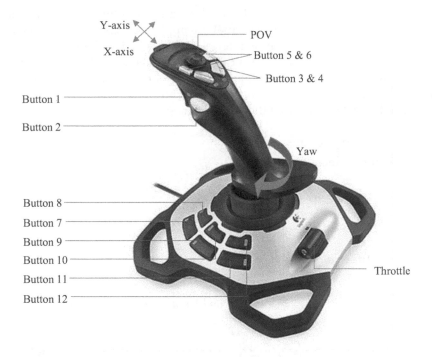

**FIGURE 2.78**

Joystick axes and buttons.

## 2.11 Data Logging

For trainees to review their performance, the simulator needs to record data from the simulation. The data logging records the position of the ROV at each time frame in a constant time interval and accumulates the data into an array. It is vital to ensure that there is a constant time interval for each frame so that the simulation would be recorded according to real time. It can be done by using time.time function in the C# script. Once the simulation is completed, the data are exported in a text file. It can be done by using a time.time static variable in the update function. The framework of data logging is shown in Figure 2.79.

## 2.12 Graphic User Interface (GUI)

The GUI provides a visual display of the simulation for user interaction. The GUI is displayed on a front panel. By applying a GameObject labeled as Canvas into Unity™ Editor interface, different UI elements such as images, text, buttons, and panels can be added as a child of the Canvas. The Canvas was set to render the UI elements in screen space – overlay, where it places the elements on the screen rendered on top of the scene. The front panel will display the following:

- Depth rating of the vehicle
- Current camera view

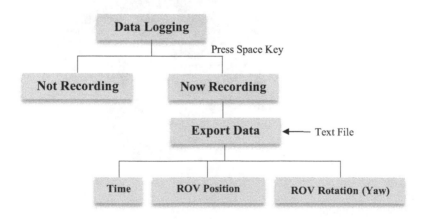

**FIGURE 2.79**
Structure of data logging.

- Speed indicator
- Total time since the simulation started
- Position of the ROV.

The UI element text is used for the camera view, speed indicator, timer, and depth rating. For the control panel, buttons and text are added as a child object to a UI panel. Figure 2.80 shows the process of developing the GUI panel, while Figures 2.81–2.84 show the overall GUI and the front panel of the GUI system from three different views.

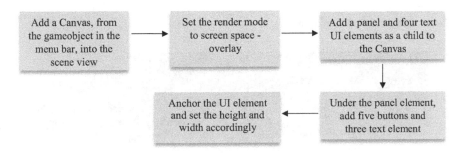

**FIGURE 2.80**
Process of creating GUI Panel.

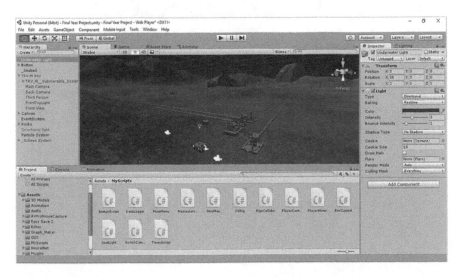

**FIGURE 2.81**
Unity's Editor Interface.

**FIGURE 2.82**
Front panel from ROV's front camera.

**FIGURE 2.83**
Front panel from ROV's back camera.

**FIGURE 2.84**
Front panel from third person view.

## 2.13 Scripting

Scripting is an essential component. It controls the physical behavior of a GameObject. It also arranges the story of the gameplay at which location and period it should happen, and also it can create graphical effects. Unity™ scripts can be written in three programming languages (JavaScript, C#, and Boo). All codings were written in C# scripts using an external script Editor called Visual Studios 2015 instead of MonoDevelop built-in external script Editor. Every script is derived from a base class called MonoBehaviour where it provides a list of functions and events that are accessible to standard scripts attached to the GameObject. The three main events that occur in a script are shown in Figure 2.85.

The Awake() and Start() functions are called automatically when the script is loaded. The only difference is for the Awake() function. It can be called when the script component is unchecked. It is called before the Start() function. These two functions are used for the initialization of codes and are used once in the life cycle.

While in the Update() and FixedUpdate() functions, the functions are called once per frame on every script. For an object that required regular changes to its position or rotation, all commands are written under these two functions. The only difference for these two is that in FixedUpdate, frames are called at a constant time interval on GameObject that has a rigidbody. There are a few different scripts required, and most of the scripts will be attached to the main GameObject in the ROV. Figure 2.86 shows a brief process on how to create a C# script. The name and function of all the scripts will be listed and described next.

### 2.13.1 RovControl

The function of RovControl script is to control the behavior of the underwater vehicle. When an input signal is received from the end-user, the script will translate these signals to different motion of the ROV.

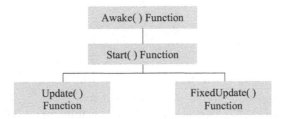

**FIGURE 2.85**
Main events on C# script.

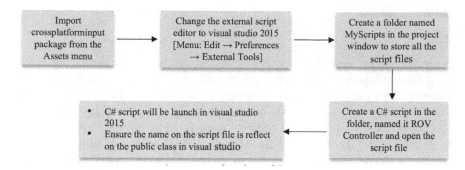

```
Import                    Change the external script          Create a folder named
crossplatforminput        editor to visual studio 2015        MyScripts in the project
package from the          [Menu: Edit → Preferences           window to store all the
Assets menu               → External Tools]                   script files
```

```
• C# script will be launch in visual studio      Create a C# script in the
  2015                                            folder, named it ROV
• Ensure the name on the script file is reflect   Controller and open the
  on the public class in visual studio            script file
```

**FIGURE 2.86**
Creating a C# script.

```
using UnityEngine;
using UnityEngine.UI;

public class RovControl : MonoBehaviour {

    //Movement
    private float fwdThruster = 1024f;
    private float revThruster = 668f;
    private float latThruster = 490f;
    private float vertThruster = 1024f;
    private float yRotationSpeed = 2.095f;
    public float fwdThrustForce;
    public float latThrustForce;
    public float vertThrustForce;
    private Rigidbody rbody;

    public Animator topProperller1;
    public Animator topProperller2;
    public Animator backProperllerL;
    public Animator backProperllerR;

    //GUI Text
    public Text depth;

    // Use this for initialization
    void Start () {
        rbody = GetComponent<Rigidbody>();
    }

    // Update is called once per frame
    void Update () {
        depth.text = "depth: " + Mathf.Round(-gameObject.transform.position.y * 10) / 10 + " m";
    }

    void FixedUpdate() {
        float power = Input.GetAxisRaw("Throttle");
        float zMove = Input.GetAxisRaw("Joystick Forward");
        float xMove = Input.GetAxisRaw("Joystick Lateral");
        float vMove = Input.GetAxisRaw("JoystickButton5&6");
        float yaw = Input.GetAxisRaw("Joystick Yaw");
```

**FIGURE 2.87**
RovControl script (Part 1).

First, some variables have to be defined in the script. From line 7 to line 10 in Figure 2.87, four private float variables are assigned to store the maximum thrust forces (forward, reverse, lateral, and vertical) of the underwater vehicle. The turning rate of the ROV, as stated in the specification sheet, is 120°/s. This value was converted to rad/s and was then assigned as a float variable under "yRotationSpeed". The three float variables for the thrust force are required. Three variables were set to the public so that they can be accessed from other scripts. Next, a variable for the rigidbody component of the GameObject is required. It is the main element that governs the motion of the ROV. Since there were animation clips attached to the propellers of the ROV, animator variables are required. Next, a GUI text element will be displayed on the front panel to update the user on the current depth of the vehicle.

When the Start() function gets called, the "rbody" variable stores the rigidbody on the GameObject, TRV-M ROV model. In the Update() function, the text variable stores a string of characters where it will be displayed on the front panel when the simulation starts. The Mathf.Round function gets hold of the GameObject transform position in y and rounds it off to one decimal place. As the GameObject has a rigidbody, all of its motion commands are called in the FixedUpdate() function. The first few items that need to be defined are the input signal, where they are assigned to different float variables. As seen in Figure 2.88, the throttle input axis will control the input power assigned to a float variable named "power".

The joystick forward and lateral input axes are assigned to "zMove" and "xMove" variables, respectively. These two input axes will control the surge and sway motion of the ROV. The 5th and 6th buttons on the joystick are assigned to the "vMove" variable as the input axis for the heave motion. Lastly, the joystick yaw axis that is the Z-Axis on the joystick is assigned to the "yaw" variable.

If a power input that is greater than zero (see Figure 2.88), it implies the user moves the Z-Axis on the joystick. It will animate the animation clips that were attached to the propellers. Thus, once the underwater vehicle receives a power input, it will cause the propeller to rotate. When the user gives an input signal, it will increase the float variables (zMove, xMove, vMove, and yaw) to positive or negative. If the "zMove" is greater than zero, the "fwdThrustForce" variable will be a product of the power input multiplied by the "fwdThruster" and the positive "zmove" input.

If the "zMove" is less than zero, the "fwdThrustForce" variable will be the product of the power input multiplied by the "revThrsuter" and the negative input from the "zMove". If the "xMove" is greater or lesser than zero, the "latThrustForce" will be the product of the power input multiplied by "latThruster" float variable and the positive or negative "xMove" input. Next, if the "vMove" is greater or lesser than zero, it will set the animator to true to animate the clips attached to the top propeller. The "vertThrustForce" variable is the product of the power input multiplied by "vertThruster" and the positive or negative input from the "vMove". However, if there is an input signal received from the 5th or 6th button on the joystick, the "vMove" becomes zero and the animator will not start.

```
if (power > 0) {
    backProperllerL.SetBool("LeftFwd", true);
    backProperllerR.SetBool("RightFwd", true);
    if (zMove > 0)
        fwdThrustForce = power * fwdThruster * zMove ;
    if (zMove < 0)
        fwdThrustForce = power * revThruster * -zMove;
    if (xMove > 0)
        latThrustForce = power * latThruster * xMove;
    if (xMove < 0)
        latThrustForce = power * latThruster * -xMove;
    if (vMove > 0) {
        topProperller1.SetBool("TFRotate", true);
        topProperller2.SetBool("TBRotate", true);
        vertThrustForce = power * vertThruster * vMove;
    }
    if (vMove < 0) {
        topProperller1.SetBool("TFRotate", true);
        topProperller2.SetBool("TBRotate", true);
        vertThrustForce = power * vertThruster * -vMove;
    }

    if (vMove == 0) {
        topProperller1.SetBool("TFRotate", false);
        topProperller2.SetBool("TBRotate", false);
    }

    Vector3 moveForward = transform.forward * zMove * fwdThrustForce;
    Vector3 moveLateral = transform.right * xMove * latThrustForce;
    Vector3 moveVertical = transform.up * vMove * vertThrustForce;

    rbody.AddForce(moveForward + moveLateral + moveVertical, ForceMode.Force);
}

else {
    backProperllerL.SetBool("LeftFwd", false);
    backProperllerR.SetBool("RightFwd", false);
}

Vector3 yRotation = new Vector3(0, yaw, 0) * yRotationSpeed;
rbody.MoveRotation(rbody.rotation * Quaternion.Euler(yRotation));
    }
}
```

**FIGURE 2.88**
RovControl script (Part 2).

Next, these variables are applied to the transform position of the ROV. The first vector3 variable is given a name as "moveForward". It is the product of the transform.forward multiplied by "zMove" input and the "fwdThrustForce". The tranform.forward is a shorthand for writing vector3 (0, 0, 1). The next vector3 variable is the "moveLateral" equal to the product of the transform.right multiplied by "xMove" input and "latThrustForce". The last vector3 variable is the "moveVertical" set as a product of the tranform.up multiplied by the "vMove" input and the "vertThrust" variable. These three variables are then applied to the ROV's rigidbody by using the addforce function in the script as shown in line 73 in Figure 2.88. If the power input if less than zero, the animation for the back propellers will not be played. These are the commands for the motion of the ROV in XYZ direction.

The last part of the script is written for the orientation of the ROV about Y-Axis. Similar to the translational motion, the orientation uses a vector3 variable. The vector3 is named as "yRotation". It is set to be a new vector (0, yaw, 0) multiplied by the "yRotationSpeed". It means that the rotation about Y-Axis gets input from the Z-Axis on the joystick and multiplied it to the rotation speed. The vector3 variable is applied to the rigidbody by using move-rotation command as shown in line 82 in Figure 2.88. The rigidbody rotation is multiplied by quanternions.euler with the vector3 variable set within its parenthesis. Quanternions.Euler is a function in Unity™ that has to be used to change the rotation of a GameObject.

### 2.13.2 SwitchCamera

The SwitchCamera script controls the rotation of the camera view (panning and tilting). It allows users to switch between cameras when a button on the joystick is being pressed. The first variable is the camera data type variable. Since the scene will consist of three cameras (main, back, and third person), the cameras are stored into three different variables, namely "camera1", "camera2", and "camera3". In line 10 of the script, an array with a variable named as "cam" is written such that it can store all the cameras. Lines 11 and 12 of the script defined the current camera (with index as zero) and the "currentCamera" will be the current camera in the scene.

Vector3 variable will be required to store the Euler angles of the cameras for rotation. A float variable for camera rotation speed is necessary as it determines how fast the camera can rotate. Lastly, a Text data type belongs to the class of the UnityEngine.UI is required. It will be displayed on the front panel to inform the trainees on the current camera view. When the Start() function is called, the "cam" array will store a new camera array as follows:

- "camera1" as the 0th index
- "camera2" as the 1st index
- "camera3" as the 2nd index.

It will store the main camera, "camera1" as the current camera. The "mainCamera" and "backCamera" are variables of a vector3. It will find the transform component that is attached to GameObject named "Main Camera" and "Back Camera" as the Euler angles of the two objects. The start function will then execute a function called ChangeView().

If it receives an input from joystick button 10, the current camera index will be increased by 1. However, if it keeps receiving inputs from the joystick, the current camera index will increase further (index number for this script is only up to two). Therefore, the scripts need to know if the current camera index is higher than the cam length. If the current camera index is greater than 2, the current camera index will be zero. Lastly, the ChangeView() function will be called once in every frame to receive input from the joystick button.

The next command is to control the rotation of the camera. If the current camera index equals 0 or 1, the vector3 variable will get the Euler angle around the X- and Y-axis. It will be increased according to the input axis multiplied by the camera rotation sensitivity. The Euler angles need to be set to a minimum and maximum value. Therefore, the camera can only rotate up to a maximum of 20° in clockwise and anti-clockwise directions. These two parameters are applied to the transform component of the "Main Camera" and "Back Camera". The script is shown in Figures 2.89 and 2.90. Based on the number of the current camera index, the "cameraText" will display the current camera name, namely

- "Camera 1" for index 0
- "Camera 2" for index 1
- "Camera 3" for index 2.

```
using UnityEngine;
using UnityEngine.UI;

public class SwitchCamera : MonoBehaviour {

    //Define Variables
    public Camera Camera1;
    public Camera Camera2;
    public Camera Camera3;
    private Camera[] cams;
    private int currentCameraIndex = 0;
    private Camera currentCamera;

    private Vector3 mainCamera;
    private Vector3 backCamera;
    private float camRotationSensitivity = 1.0f;
    public Text cameraText;

    void Start () {
        cams = new Camera[] { Camera1, Camera2, Camera3 };
        currentCamera = Camera1;
        mainCamera = transform.Find("Main Camera").eulerAngles;
        backCamera = transform.Find("Back Camera").eulerAngles;
        ChangeView();
    }

    void Update() {
        if (Input.GetKeyDown(KeyCode.JoystickButton10)) {
            currentCameraIndex++;
            if (currentCameraIndex > cams.Length - 1)
                currentCameraIndex = 0;
            ChangeView();
        }

        if (currentCameraIndex == 0) {
            mainCamera.x += Input.GetAxisRaw("Joystick Hat Y") * camRotationSensitivity;
            mainCamera.y += Input.GetAxisRaw("Joystick Hat X") * camRotationSensitivity;
            mainCamera.x = Mathf.Clamp(mainCamera.x, -20, 20);
            mainCamera.y = Mathf.Clamp(mainCamera.y, -20, 20);
            transform.Find("Main Camera").localRotation = Quaternion.Euler(-mainCamera.x, mainCamera.y, 0);
            cameraText.text = "Camera 1";
        }
    }
```

**FIGURE 2.89**
SwitchCamera (Part 1).

```
        if (currentCameraIndex == 1) {
            backCamera.x += Input.GetAxisRaw("Joystick Hat Y") * camRotationSensitivity;
            backCamera.y += Input.GetAxisRaw("Joystick Hat X") * camRotationSensitivity;
            backCamera.x = Mathf.Clamp(backCamera.x, -20, 20);
            backCamera.y = Mathf.Clamp(backCamera.y, 160, 200);
            transform.Find("Back Camera").localRotation = Quaternion.Euler(-backCamera.x, backCamera.y, 0);
            cameraText.text = "Camera 2";
        }

        if (currentCameraIndex == 2)
            cameraText.text = "Camera 3";
    }

    void ChangeView() {
        currentCamera.enabled = false;
        currentCamera = cams[currentCameraIndex];
        currentCamera.enabled = true;
    }
}
```

**FIGURE 2.90**
SwitchCamera (Part 2).

### 2.13.3 Manipulators

The Manipulators script controls the ROV's manipulators. The animator controller has a parameter to animate the video clips when a true or false command is given. Two primitive box colliders were attached to the jaws of the manipulators. The script is written such that when the user clicks on a GUI button (on/off), it will activate the true or false command. The animator controller can animate the clips. At the same time, it will enable the box collider on the jaws. The script also allows users to control the rotation of the jaws using a few buttons on the keyboard. The script is shown in Figures 2.91 and 2.92. The script is attached to TRV-M ROV.

The part of the script is to define all the variables required, for example, a public scope for the GUI button on the front panel, the animation of the manipulators, the transform position of the jaw and the GameObjects. The private float variables are used to store the maximum and minimum values of the jaw rotation and the speed of rotation.

As the jaw of the manipulators needs to be changed regularly on a constant time interval, the command is executed in the "FixedUpdate" function. When the FixedUpdate function is called, the rightJawRotation and leftJawRotation will receive an increment that is equal to the input axis multiplied by the rotation rate. The "Right Manipulator" and "Left Manipulator" are simply I, P, Q, and E keycodes defined in the input manager. In addition, the two float variables are set to a minimum of −90 and a maximum of 90. It means that each jaw can rotate 90° clockwise and anticlockwise. The float variables are then applied to the rightJaw and leftJaw. Therefore, when the FixedUpdate is called, the manipulator jaws will rotate based on the input received from the end-user. The maximum rotation is therefore 90° to the left or right.

The last part of the script is written for the activation/deactivation of the manipulators. When the end-user presses the "On" button on the

```
using UnityEngine;
using UnityEngine.UI;

public class Manipulators : MonoBehaviour {

    //Manipulators Activation & Deactivation
    public Button Activate;
    public Button Deactivate;
    public Animator rightManipulator;
    public Animator leftManipulator;

    //Manipulator Controls
    public Transform rightJaw;
    public Transform leftJaw;
    private float rightJawRotation;
    private float leftJawRotation;
    private float minJawRotation = -90f;
    private float maxJawRotation = 90f;
    private float rotationRate = 2f;
    public GameObject rightArm;
    public GameObject leftArm;

    // Update is called once per frame
    void FixedUpdate() {
        rightJawRotation += Input.GetAxis("Right Jaw") * rotationRate;
        rightJawRotation = Mathf.Clamp(rightJawRotation, minJawRotation, maxJawRotation);
        rightJaw.eulerAngles = new Vector3(rightJawRotation, rightJaw.eulerAngles.y, rightJaw.eulerAngles.z);

        leftJawRotation += Input.GetAxis("Left Jaw") * rotationRate;
        leftJawRotation = Mathf.Clamp(leftJawRotation, minJawRotation, maxJawRotation);
        leftJaw.eulerAngles = new Vector3(leftJawRotation, leftJaw.eulerAngles.y, leftJaw.eulerAngles.z);

    }

    //To open the ROV Manipulator (R)
    public void onPressRight (){
        rightManipulator.SetBool("rightOpen", true);
        Collider rightArmCollider = rightArm.GetComponent<Collider>();
        rightArmCollider.enabled = true;
    }
```

**FIGURE 2.91**
Manipulators script (Part 1).

```
    //To close the ROV Manipulator (R)
    public void offPressRight (){
        rightManipulator.SetBool("rightOpen", false);
        Collider rightArmCollider = rightArm.GetComponent<Collider>();
        rightArmCollider.enabled = false;
    }
    //To open the ROV Manipulator (L)
    public void onPressLeft () {
        leftManipulator.SetBool("leftOpen", true);
        Collider leftArmCollider = leftArm.GetComponent<Collider>();
        leftArmCollider.enabled = true;
    }

    //To close the ROV Manipulator (L)
    public void offPressLeftt() {
        leftManipulator.SetBool("leftOpen", false);
        Collider leftArmCollider = leftArm.GetComponent<Collider>();
        leftArmCollider.enabled = false;
    }
}
```

**FIGURE 2.92**
Manipulators script (Part 2).

front panel, it will run the "onPress" function in this script. It will set the parameter on "rightManipulator" or "leftManipulator", depending on which "On" button is pressed. The collider variable will get the collider component in the manipulators to true. The "offPress" function works similarly to cause the manipulators to rotate back.

## 2.13.4 Spotlight

The Spotlight script allows the user to switch on and off the power light system on the ROV model by using a button on the joystick. The script will be attached to the Spotlight GameObject as a child of the TRV-M ROV. The commands written in the Spotlight script are shown in Figure 2.93.

As the Spotlight does not require a regular update, the commands will be written under the Update() function. The control input for the Spotlight will be button number 2 on the joystick. However, the keycode in Unity3D starts with an index 0. The keycode for button number 2 on the joystick will be joystick button 1. If a key input from the joystick is received, the script will change the light component on the GameObject. Otherwise, the light component on the GameObject will change the light component to true.

## 2.13.5 Timer Script

The timer script is used to inform the user of the current time taken after the simulation is executed. The script is shown in Figure 2.94.

Since the timer will be displayed on the GUI panel, the script requires UnityEngine.UI function. The UnityEngine.UI provides a list of classes and variables that can be accessed from the script. The first variable that was defined in the script is the "timer". A GUI timer text element was created in the front panel.

When the Start() function is called, the "startTimer" will store the time. time in seconds as soon as the simulation is executed. Therefore, the "startTimer" will store the time taken for the start function to initialize all its variables. Note that the Start() function is called once. In the Update() function, a float variable "t" stores a time.time value without taking into account the time taken to execute the Start() function. The variable "t" only stores the time in seconds as soon as the Update() function is being

```
using UnityEngine;
using System.Collections;

public class SpotLight : MonoBehaviour {

    // Update is called once per frame
    void Update () {
        if (Input.GetKeyDown(KeyCode.JoystickButton1))
        {
            if (GetComponent<Light>().enabled == false)
            {
                GetComponent<Light>().enabled = true;
            }
            else
            {
                GetComponent<Light>().enabled = false;
            }
        }
    }
}
```

**FIGURE 2.93**
Spotlight script.

```
using UnityEngine;
using System.Collections;
using UnityEngine.UI;

public class TimerScript : MonoBehaviour {

    public Text timer;
    private float startTimer;

    // Use this for initialization
    void Start () {
        startTimer = Time.time;
    }

    // Update is called once per frame
    void Update () {

        float t = Time.time - startTimer;

        string seconds = (t % 60).ToString("f1");
        timer.text = "Time: " + seconds +" s";
    }
}
```

**FIGURE 2.94**
Timer script.

executed. A variable "seconds" of a string data type stores the variable "t" and converts it to a string. The timer.text will then display a string "Time:" plus the seconds followed by "s" string that represents the unit of the time.

### 2.13.6 DataLogger

A DataLogger script is used to record the position of the ROV and the time taken by the trainee during the simulation. It records the position of the ROV at every frame in a constant time interval as an array. It is essential to ensure that there is a constant time interval at every frame. Once the simulation is completed, the data are exported in a text file. It can be performed using a time.time static variable in the update function.

A TextWriter variable is needed as the main function for data exporting. The TextWriter is a class of the System.IO. Thus, it needs to be defined at the top of the script. Two variables of a string data type are required. Next, the data logging is set for the user to press a keycode. Lines 11 and 12 in Figure 2.95 are integer variables where the "recordNumber" was set to −1 and the "last" was set to 0.

The GameObject is required such that the script can store its transform position and Euler angle. The data logger script can access variables from the RovControl script. Thus, it is defined as a public variable where the RovControl script can be included in the Inspector window. This script can access the float variable of the forward, lateral, and vertical thrust forces defined in lines 16–18. Note that a float variable is used to store the time taken for the Start() function.

```
using UnityEngine;
using System.IO;

public class DataLogger : MonoBehaviour {

    //Text Results
    TextWriter tw;
    string resultText;
    bool isRecording = false;
    string fileName;
    int recordNumber = -1;
    int last = 0;

    public GameObject rov;
    public RovControl rovScript;
    public float fwdThrust;
    public float latThrust;
    public float verThrust;
    float time;

    Vector3 rovCurrentPos = Vector3.zero;
    Vector3 rovCurrentRot = Vector3.zero;

    public static float[] DeltaData = new float[7];

    // Use this for initialization
    void Start() {
        time = Time.time;
    }

    void Update () {
        float timeTaken = Time.time - time;
        string t = timeTaken.ToString("f3");
        rovScript = rov.GetComponent<RovControl>();
        fwdThrust = rovScript.fwdThrustForce;
        latThrust = rovScript.latThrustForce;
        verThrust = rovScript.vertThrustForce;
        rovCurrentPos = rov.transform.localPosition;
        rovCurrentRot = rov.transform.eulerAngles;
```

**FIGURE 2.95**
DataLogger script (Part 1).

When the Start() function is executed, the time variable can store the time.time. It is the time taken in seconds after the simulation starts. A float variable (timeTaken) will store the time.time. However, it will not include the time taken in the start function. The "timeTaken" variable will only store the time taken to run all the commands in the Update() function. A string variable "t" will convert the "timeTaken" variable into a string variable with three decimal places.

The "rovScript" variable will get the script component from the ROV GameObject and the "fwdThrust", "latThrust", and "verThrust", in the data logger script. The vector3 variables, "rovCurrentPos" and "rovCurrentRot", will get the transform component in the GameObject to store its local position and Euler angle, respectively. The local position in XYZ, Euler angle around Y-Axis, and the three thrust force will be stored in "DeltaData". It will be executed in a loop where the commands are repeated (see Figure 2.96). These data are then stored in the "resultText" for the TextWriter.

If the Update() function received a key input (space bar) by the user, it would set the "isRecording" equal to true. The recordNumber will be increased by 1. If "isRecording" is equal to true, it will print ("now

```
int i = 0;
for (i = 0; i<100; i++) {
    if(i == 99) {
        DeltaData[0] = rovCurrentPos.x;
        DeltaData[1] = rovCurrentPos.y;
        DeltaData[2] = rovCurrentPos.z;
        DeltaData[3] = rovCurrentRot.y;
        DeltaData[4] = fwdThrust;
        DeltaData[5] = latThrust;
        DeltaData[6] = verThrust;
    }
}

resultText = DeltaData[0] + "\t " + DeltaData[1] + "\t " + DeltaData[2] + "\t" + DeltaData[3] +
    "\t" + DeltaData[4] + "\t" + DeltaData[5] + "\t" + DeltaData[6] + "\t" + t;

if (Input.GetKeyDown(KeyCode.Space)) {
    if (isRecording) {
        recordNumber++;
    }
    isRecording = !isRecording;
}

if (isRecording) {
    print("now recording!");
    if (last != recordNumber){
        fileName = "Results.txt";
        tw = new Streamwriter(fileName);
        last = recordNumber;
    }
    WriteFile();
}
else {
    print("Not Recording");
}
}

void WriteFile () {
    tw.WriteLine(resultText);
    tw.Flush();
}
```

**FIGURE 2.96**
DataLogger script (Part 2).

recording!") on the Editor's console. If the "last" variable is not equal to the "recordNumber", the "fileName" will be changed to "Results.txt". The TextWriter variable will store a new streamwriter with the "fileName" variable in its parenthesis. The "last" variable will be equal to the "recordNumber". At the end, the Update() function will be executed. In the WriteFile() function, the tw.WriteLine writes a line terminator to the text string that is the "resultText" and tw.Flush. It clears all the buffers for the current write.

## 2.13.7 ButtonScript

A scenario is set up where there is a leakage in one of the jumpers at the top section. Thus, to stop the leakage, the ROV has to shut down the system. The ButtonScript is written such that when the ROV jaws touch the tip of the button, it will activate the OnTrigger function to deactivate the system by animating a pushing clip of the button. A text stating "System has been shut down" will be shown on the front panel. The script is shown in Figure 2.97.

```
using UnityEngine;
using System.Collections;
using UnityEngine.UI;

public class ButtonScript : MonoBehaviour {

    public Animator button;
    public Text mission;
    public GameObject gasParticle;

    void OnTriggerEnter(Collider rovJaw) {
        button.SetBool("Activate Button", true);

        gasParticle.gameObject.SetActive(false);
        mission.text = "System has been shut down!";
    }
}
```

**FIGURE 2.97**
ButtonScript.

The button was attached with an animation clip to store the button to activate the animation. A text variable is a class of the UnityEngine. UI to store the mission text. The last variable would be a GameObject variable named ParticleSystem. The command will be done in OnTriggerEnter() function. As stated, there is a box collider placed around the button and its parameter is set as isTrigger. When the jaw collider of the ROV enters the box collider, it will set the button animation to true to animate the clip.

At the same time, the gasParticle as a GameObject will be set to false. The GameObject is disabled from the game scene. A mission text will be shown on the front panel with a statement ("System has been shut down!") to acknowledge trainees that the system has successfully shut down.

**FIGURE 2.98**
All scripts used in ROV.

*Intelligent Virtual System*

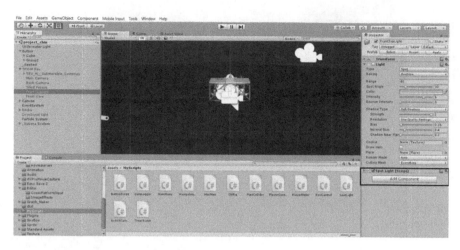

**FIGURE 2.99**
Spotlight script used in ROV.

All the scripts used in TRV-M ROV Model can be summarized as follows. The use of the scripts is shown in Figure 2.98, where the TRV-M ROV is using it for controlling the camera, manipulators, timing, and data collection.

- RovControl.cs
- SwitchCamera.cs
- Manipulators.cs
- Timer Script.cs
- Data Logger.cs

In addition, another two scripts used for TRV-M ROV and Button are as follows:

- SpotLight.cs (see Figure 2.99)
- ButtonScript.cs (see Figure 2.100).

Finally, under the menu, select File → Build & Run to create an application file (in exe) as shown in Figure 2.101. The file can be executed and run as shown in Figure 2.101. The final outlook of the animation is shown in Figure 2.102.

The details of all the scripts used can be found in Appendix D. Note that the naming of the scripts depends on the users.

**FIGURE 2.100**
Button script used in ROV.

**FIGURE 2.101**
Build & Run to create application file.

**FIGURE 2.102**
Virtual ROV performing pipeline inspection in 3D.

# 3

## Results and Discussion

### 3.1 Virtual Simulation Results with Videos

The simulation test results focus on pipeline inspection tasks near to the seabed. The different parts in developing the simulation are integrated with a scenario where there exists a gas leakage in one of the pipelines. The data for the search operation are exported and plotted into a graph. The results obtained are shown in Figures 3.1–3.3. First, the ROV will ascend to the required depth, as shown in Figure 3.2. The ROV will ascend to the depth (x = 0 m, y = 0 m, z = −793 m) that is at the center of the subsea production layout. The ROV then rotates about its Y-Axis in an anti-clockwise direction shown in Figure 3.3 where the ROV's heading is facing approximately 190° away from its global coordinate before it starts moving in X and Z directions again. The ROV moves along at a constant depth of −793 m for approximately 38 seconds before it moves up to avoid colliding onto the seabed.

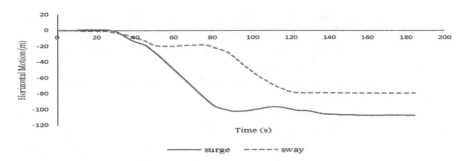

**FIGURE 3.1**
X and Y positions of ROV at different time frames.

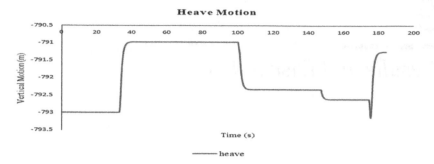

**FIGURE 3.2**
Z position of ROV at various time frames.

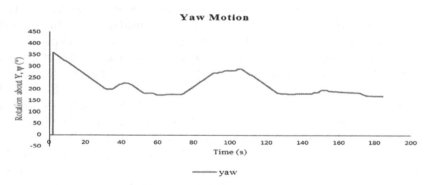

**FIGURE 3.3**
Yaw angle of ROV at various time frames.

Second, the next task is to identify the location of the leakage, as seen in Figure 3.4. As observed in Figures 3.5–3.7, the forward, lateral, and vertical thrusts (in N) produced by the ROV increase to reach the targeted position. The thrusts decrease once it is near to the leakage. There is less fluctuating in the motion along the X, Z-Axes, and changes in the orientation about Y-Axis.

Lastly, the ROV will need to deactivate the whole system by pressing the switch on the BOP using the manipulators in Figure 3.8. The position of the ROV increases along the Z-Axis while its location along the X-Axis remains quite constant. The ROV rotates clockwise about the Y-Axis to approximately 200° at 87 seconds, where the position of the ROV increases along the X-Axis and remains quite constant on the Z-Axis. After approximately 140 seconds later, the ROV has deactivated the BOP system to prevent any further leakage. In Figure 3.8, the left manipulator of the ROV is used to shut down the subsea system. It can be seen that the ROV

**FIGURE 3.4**
Leakage found in pipeline.

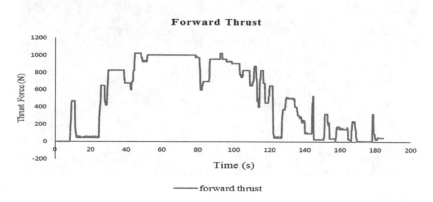

**FIGURE 3.5**
Total forward thrust at different time frames.

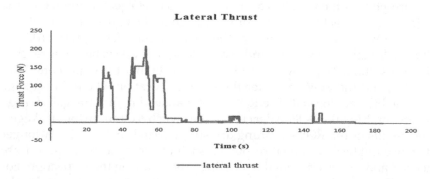

**FIGURE 3.6**
Total lateral thrust at various time frames.

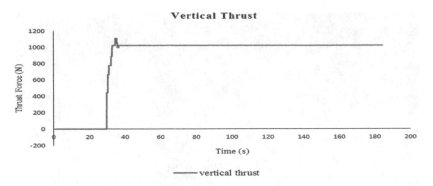

**FIGURE 3.7**
Total vertical thrust at different time frames.

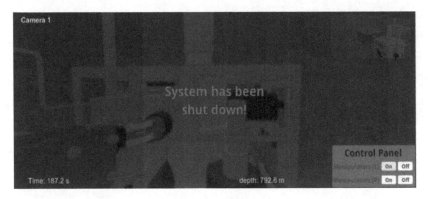

**FIGURE 3.8**
Subsea system deactivated.

is at the targeted position to close the system after about 190 seconds. With the presence of the colliders around every GameObject in the scene, the objects can interact with one another though in the real environment.

The ROV starting position is at the center section facing forward. The ROV will make a few turns and move along the X-Axis before it reaches the top section. The movement of ROV reflects that the data plotted are reliable, and the ROV can enter the targeted location where the leakage and the BOP are located. The ROV pilot managed to find the gas leakage before reaching the BOP to deactivate the switch to stop further leakages. The results of the ROV's training are summarized in Table 3.1. A longer distance implies additional resources such as more electrical power are needed and diversion from the pipeline profile during the inspection. For example, it can deviate from the pipeline, or the distance moves by the

**TABLE 3.1**

ROV Pilot Training Report – Results from one ROV Pilot Trainee

| Descriptions | Results |
| --- | --- |
| Total distance traveled in X direction | 79.29 m |
| Total distance traveled in Y direction | 73.10 m |
| Total distance traveled in Z direction | 107.27 m |
| Final heave position | −792.57 m |
| Final heading angle | 169.75° |
| Total time taken | 202.18 s |
| Obstacle hits | 0 |
| Gas leakage found | 1 |
| Subsea system deactivated | 1 |

ROV in Y-direction is higher. A shorter time (conversely, a shorter total distance traveled) taken to complete the task is often desired. However, it should not compromise the safety, such as hitting an obstacle and taking a shortcut without inspecting the pipeline to achieve a shorter mission time. The proposed serious game approach allows the same pilot or other trainees to practice repeatedly, and provide feedback to action as shown in Table 3.1. The challenges involve shorter mission time, a lesser number of obstacles hit, shorter distance traveled to find the leakage and shut down the BOP. The trainees can repeat the game to improve their scores or compete with one another.

In summary, the use of open-source virtual reality game engine software when coupled with the use of a joystick device enables a low-cost solution to ROV pilot training. Thus, VR offers an increase in the human–machine interface, the mobility of such system, and entertainment to trainees via a serious gaming environment. The amount of story depending on the type of situation, user interaction for decision making, and rules can be easily incorporated into the game environment for further fine-tuning of the ROV pilot training. However, the disadvantage is that it may take time for the maritime industry to embrace using the serious game engine for ROV pilot training purposes. As stated in the earlier section, the objective of this book is to develop an ROV simulation using a low-cost and off-the-shelf development tool. The results obtained have shown that Unity3D has the capability of developing a good visual stimulation.

The recorded videos of the completed virtual simulator performing the tasks can be seen on the following websites:

- Setup: https://www.youtube.com/watch?v=vIjLfBF3soo
- Training: https://www.youtube.com/watch?v=PNyD1qRLCYU

## 3.2 User Experience Study of ROV Pilot Simulator

A user study can be developed. The purposes are to determine (a) whether or not certain aspects of ROV pilot situational performance and (b) user experience can be enhanced by the game-based ROV pilot simulator as compared to a commercial VR simulator such as ROVsim$^2$Pro developed using a different game engine. The time and cost to market and mobility of the proposed ROV pilot training system are improved by using the open-source Unity3D, and the mobile wearable VR Gear will not be included.

### 3.2.1 Participants

The participants consisted of mainly students. They were chosen as they were working on engineering projects, and it is quite easy to engage them. Another reason is that it is hard to use professional ROV pilot trainees in the study as they need to be paid hourly that is beyond the budget of this study. However, if the results of the user study are shown to be positive, the simulator can be further improved, and an extensive research involving the professional can be sought in the future. The study consisted of 20 individuals (10 females and 10 males) between the ages of 20 and 24. The 20 selected participants did not experience the same ROV pilot simulator that helps to prevent any experimenter bias. However, the participants had some experiences of playing games through their smartphones and have been explained on how to operate the VR simulator. Besides, another ten participants (all males aged 35–50 years) with experience in gaming and aerospace training simulator were used in the user study. All 30 participants were restricted to 10 minutes in the simulation to prevent simulator sickness.

The participants will be judged based on the pipeline inspection performance using different software such as the proposed ROV pilot simulator and ROVsim$^2$Pro. They are namely small deviations of search path from the ideal pipeline layout, mission time, obstacle hit, identification of leakage, and the ability to shut down the subsea system. However, it has to be noted that the operating console of the ROVsim$^2$Pro is slightly more complicated as it is commercial software, virtual equipment is different, and the seabed design is different.

In addition, the user experience such as realism, quality of the interface, the possibility to act, the possibility to examine, self-evaluation, and sound in the questionnaire will need to be completed. The participants were given instructions to complete the result sheet and the user experience questionnaire.

### 3.2.2 ROV Pilot Situational Performance

The results of the root mean squared error from the ideal search path show that there is a difference in the results for a different scenario using various start locations of ROV. The errors are higher for the female participants as compared to the male. The mission time can be seen to have a wider difference in female students and has a longer time as compared to the male participants. The number of times the obstacle hit is quite high as the participants are trying to keep the ROV in the correct orientations during the pipeline inspection. The identification of the leakage and shutdown of the system depends very much on how well the participants can maintain a stable orientation of the ROV during the inspection and the time it spends at the initial stage of the game. In general, most of the participants can detect the leakage except a few participants. As compared to the proposed ROV pilot simulator to ROVsim$^2$Pro, the following t-test results for the pipeline tracking accuracy, mission time, and obstacle hit indicate that the mean difference is significant at the range of 10–17% level, returning a P-value of less than 0.05. The results in Table 3.2 show an increase (or different) in the pipeline tracking accuracy, mission time, and obstacle hit as compared to the identification of leakage and deactivation of the system. The standard error of the mean estimates the variability between samples. It can be seen that the error of the mean is quite small. Hence, the mean of the differences between the proposed ROV pilot simulator and ROVsim$^2$Pro is statistically significant for the pipeline tracking accuracy, mission time, and obstacle hit. In general, the ROVsim$^2$Pro gives a slightly lower accuracy and a longer mission time, but a lower obstacle hit.

### 3.3 Questionnaire

A questionnaire was used to assess the user experience during the simulations. The questions were divided into six categories using the verified French Canadian method of evaluation. These classes included (1) realism, (2) possibility to act, (3) quality of the interface, (4) possibility to examine, (5) self-evaluation of performance, and (6) sounds. In this study, statistical analysis was performed on these categories to compare the various levels (from 1 to 5) using the following ranking:

- 1 indicates very dissatisfied
- 2 indicates dissatisfied

**TABLE 3.2**

t-Test for Comparing Mean Difference between Proposed ROV Pilot Simulator and ROVsim$^2$Pro

| Parameters | Software | Number of Samples | Mean | Standard Deviation | Standard Error of the Mean | 95% CI for Mean Difference | t-Test of Mean Difference |
|---|---|---|---|---|---|---|---|
| Pipeline tracking accuracy | Proposed ROV pilot simulator | 30 | 260.600 | 26.810 | 4.895 | (−19.3151, −13.8849) | t-Value = −12.50 P-Value = 0.0001 |
| | ROVsim$^2$Pro | 30 | 277.200 | 27.481 | 5.017 | | |
| Mission time | Proposed ROV pilot simulator | 30 | 226.167 | 24.042 | 4.389 | (−21.9520, −17.1814) | t-Value = −16.78 P-Value = 0.0001 |
| | ROVsim$^2$Pro | 30 | 245.733 | 26.451 | 4.829 | | |
| Obstacle hit | Proposed ROV pilot simulator | 30 | 8.0000 | 3.0513 | 0.5571 | (−6.85969, −4.60698) | t-Value = −10.41 P-Value = 0.0001 |
| | ROVsim$^2$Pro | 30 | 13.7333 | 4.2745 | 0.7804 | | |
| Identification of leakage | Proposed ROV pilot simulator | 30 | 0.966667 | 0.182574 | 0.033333 | (−0.034841, 0.101508) | t-Value = 1.00 P-Value = 0.326 |
| | ROVsim$^2$Pro | 30 | 0.933333 | 0.253708 | 0.046321 | | |
| Deactivate the system | Proposed ROV pilot simulator | 30 | 0.900000 | 0.305129 | 0.055709 | (−0.013937, 0.213937) | t-Value = 1.80 P-Value = 0.083 |
| | ROVsim$^2$Pro | 30 | 0.800000 | 0.406838 | 0.074278 | | |

- 3 indicates ok
- 4 indicates satisfied
- 5 indicates very satisfied.

A one-way ANOVA test was conducted with the software as the independent variable (i.e., response) and the six classes of the dependent variables (i.e., factors). The one-way ANOVA assumes homogeneity of variance. Table 3.3 shows all classes were the statistically significant difference between the software. Statistical significance was found using $\alpha$ value of 0.05. As shown in Table 3.3, the results demonstrate that it is not statistically significant differences in all classes. Figures 3.9–3.11 also indicate that the users exposed to quite similar experiences from the two software. The results were not very different as the users have seldom played computer games and exposed to commercial ROV virtual simulator.

In summary, the use of serious game-based virtual reality for ROV pilot training will bring an increased area to work on. It is easier to completely visualize and have an overview of the ROV in the real working environment with less risk. However, considerations are required while developing a training application for VR. Focusing on simplicity and avoiding complex menus by utilizing the head tracking and the 360° views using Gear VR could provide a natural feeling with easier navigation for the actual application. It is vital to model the 3D ROV's environment with high-quality textures and models for the best experience for the trainees. The adoption of the proposed serious game-based VR technology is much easier for younger users as compared to older users, where they might feel the platform is quite fast for them to react. The results suggest that it is quite comparable to the expensive commercial ROV pilot training platform.

**TABLE 3.3**

One-Way ANOVA for Proposed ROV Pilot Simulator and ROVsim$^2$Pro

| Descriptions | Degree of Freedom | Sum of Square | Mean of Square | F-value | P-value |
| --- | --- | --- | --- | --- | --- |
| Realism | 4 | 0.317 | 0.079 | 0.300 | 0.879 |
| Quality of interface | 4 | 0.925 | 0.231 | 0.900 | 0.468 |
| Possibility to act | 4 | 1.473 | 0.368 | 1.500 | 0.216 |
| Possibility to examine | 4 | 0.543 | 0.136 | 0.52 | 0.724 |
| Self-evaluation | 4 | 0.671 | 0.168 | 0.64 | 0.633 |
| Sound | 4 | 1.243 | 0.311 | 1.24 | 0.304 |

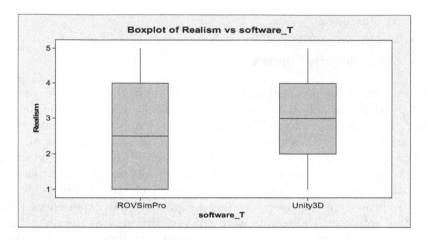

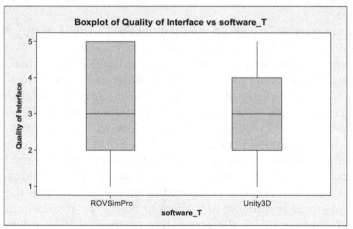

**FIGURE 3.9**
Comparison of realism and quality of interface using different software.

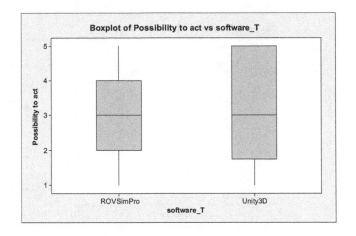

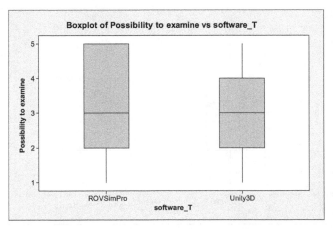

**FIGURE 3.10**
Comparison of possibility to act and possibility to examine for different types of software.

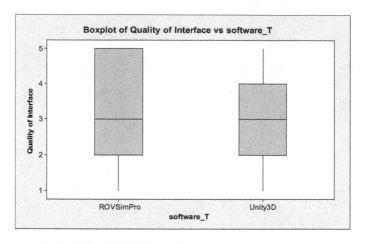

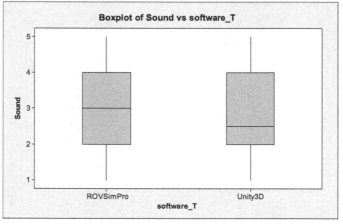

**FIGURE 3.11**
Comparison of quality of interface and sound using different types of software.

# 4

## *Conclusion*

The use of underwater vehicles such as remotely operated vehicles (ROVs) for search operation has increased. The key in performing these missions successfully lies within the skill and knowledge of the pilot. By developing a virtual simulator and implementing it as part of the training system, it would not only accelerate the pilot's progress, but it reduces the risk of damaging expansive field equipment. Although training simulators for ROV pilots are available in the market, these bespoke simulators are often very costly. Presently, there is a high interest in engaging modern game engine software as a foundation tool to develop a "serious game" as a training system.

This book has successfully demonstrated the process and merits of developing a virtual simulator using an open-source game engine to develop "serious game" for ROV pilot training using existing gaming controllers on a standard laptop. By integrating different GameObjects using event-driven programming within the development software, the proposed modern game engine is capable of producing an appropriate level of accuracy in a shorter time and lower cost than another virtual reality simulator. The mean of the differences between the proposed ROV pilot simulator and ROVsim$^2$Pro is statistically significant for the pipeline tracking accuracy, mission time, and obstacle hit. The ROVsim$^2$Pro shows lower precision, longer mission time, but smaller obstacle hit. By comparing the users' experience in realism, the possibility to act, quality of the interface, the opportunity to examine, and self-evaluation of performance and sound, the statistic results suggest that it is quite comparable to commercial ROV pilot training platform.

In summary, the proposed ROV pilot training using a serious gaming approach enhances the current ROV training capability and workplace safety in an uncertain environment. It also reduces maintenance costs as compared to full commercial ROV's pilot training. However, there are some aspects, as mention previously, that need further research so that it can be implemented into the simulation to produce a better level of accuracy in terms of physics and psychological fidelity.

# Appendix A: TRV-M ROV Technical Specification Sheet

## TRV-M

**General Specifications:**
Depth Rating ................................. 3300 ft. (1000m) standard
(deeper options)
Payload ........................................................... 60 lbs. (27 kg)
Height ............................................................ 24 in. (610 mm)
Length ............................................................ 60 in. (1524 mm)
Width .............................................................. 48 in. (1219 mm)
Weight in Air .............................................. 940 lbs. (426.37 kg)

**Maximum Static Thrust:**
Forward ........................................................................ 230 lbs.
Reverse ......................................................................... 150 lbs.
Lateral .......................................................................... 110 lbs.
Vertical ......................................................................... 230 lbs.

**Maximum Velocity: (100 ft. tether excursion)**
Forward .......................................................... 2.04 m/s (4 kts)
Reverse ........................................................... 1.53 m/s (3 kts)
Lateral ............................................................ 1.02 m/s (2 kts)
Vertical ............................................................... Up to 3 m/s
Turning Rate ............................................... 120° per second max.

**Surface Control Unit:**
Height ............................................................ 12.28 in. (312 mm)
Width .............................................................. 16.50 in. (419 mm)
Depth .............................................................. 22.25 in. (565 mm)
Weight ........................................................... 291 lbs. (132 kg)
SCU Power Requirements ............................. 220 VAC 3Ø 25kw

**Tether Dimensions:**
Tether (standard length–live boat mode) ........... 1500 ft. (500 m)
Diameter.......................................................... 22.5 mm (.886 in.)
Weight in Air ................................................. 345 lb/kft (513 kg/km)
Weight in Seawater ...................................... 71 lb/kft (106 kg/km)
Breaking Load .............................................................. 2500 lbf

**Thruster Technology:**
5 x Brushless DC motors with internal drive modules.

**Chassis:**
T6061 Aluminum

**Buoyancy:**
1000m Syntactic Foam (standard, deeper options available)

**Hand Control Unit:**
Height ................................................................... 3.25 in.
Width .................................................................... 8.5 in.
Length .................................................................. 12.0 in.
Weight ................................................................... 5.0 lbs. (2.27 kg)

**Hand Control Functions:**
Thruster Control: Fore, Aft, Lateral, Vertical, Rotate
0-100% Gain Control on Port, Stb. & Lateral
0-100% Gain Control on Verticals
0-100% Gain Control on Forward Bias
Auto Depth, Auto Heading, Auto Altitude
Thruster enable/disable
Normal/Pitch Mode Switch
Cameras: Pan, Tilt, Zoom & Focus on Colour Camera
Pan, Tilt Fixed Focus Colour Camera
Manipulator Colour Camera
Remote Control for aft 360° Colour Rotate
Camera
Manipulators: 2 x 4 Function
Swing Left/Right
Arm Up/Down
Jaw Rotate CW/CCW
Jaw Open/Close
Lights: 2 x LED Light potentiometers 0-100% intensity

**Remote Hand Control Unit:**
Height ................................................................... 2.25 in.
Width .................................................................... 7.75 in.
Depth .................................................................... 4.75 in.
Weight ................................................................... 1.0 lbs.

**Remote Hand Control Functions:**
Thruster Control: Fore, Aft, Lateral, Vertical, Rotate, Thruster
Enable/Disable Switch. Lights: On/Off (Full Intensity)

**Sonar:**
MS 1000 Sonar Head

**Modular Components:**
Telemetry Can, Power Can, Capacitor Bottle, HPU,
2 x 4-Function Valve Pack

**Navigation:**
Gyro/Fluxgate Combination w/pitch & roll.

**Lighting:**
5 x LED High Power Light Systems

**Auto Functions:**
Auto Depth, Heading & Altitude

**Cameras: 4**
Sony Color Zoom, Focus, Pan & Tilt
Low Light Colour, Pan & Tilt
Rotary Color 360° Viewing
Colour Manip Camera
Cameras on two Video OCT's (any combination of two cameras can
be viewed at any time)

Submersible Systems, Inc. P.O. Box 1843 / 333 Progresso Road, Patterson, LA 70392/ 985-395-0999/ www.ssirovs.com

See link: http://ssirovs.com/wp-content/uploads/2018/02/TRV-M_Specs.pdf

# Appendix B: Functions of the Properties Used in Unity™

| Property | Function |
|---|---|
| Axes | Contain all the defined input axes for the current project: Size is the number of different input axes in this project; Elements 0, 1... are the particular axes to modify. |
| Name | The string that refers to the axis in the game launcher and through scripting. |
| Descriptive Name | A detailed definition of the Positive Button function that is displayed in the game launcher. |
| Descriptive Negative Name | A detailed definition of the Negative Button function that is displayed in the game launcher. |
| Negative Button | The button that will send a negative value to the axis. |
| Positive Button | The button that will send a positive value to the axis. |
| Alt Negative Button | The secondary button that will send a negative value to the axis. |
| Alt Positive Button | The secondary button that will send a positive value to the axis. |
| Gravity | How fast will the input re-center. Only used when the Type is key/mouse button. |
| Dead | Any positive or negative values that are less than this number will register as zero. Useful for joysticks. |
| Sensitivity | For keyboard input, a larger value will result in faster response time. A lower value will be smoother. For Mouse delta, the value will scale the actual mouse delta. |
| Snap | If enabled, the axis value will be immediately reset to zero after it receives opposite inputs. Only used when the Type is key/mouse button. |
| Invert | If enabled, the positive buttons will send negative values to the axis, and vice versa. |
| Type | Use Key/Mouse Button for any kind of buttons, Mouse Movement for mouse delta and scrollwheels, Joystick Axis for analog joystick axes, and Window Movement for when the user shakes the window. |
| Axis | Axis of input from the device (joystick, mouse, gamepad). |
| Joy Number | Which joystick should be used. By default, this is set to retrieve the input from all joysticks. This is only used for input axes and not buttons. |

Properties of Light Window (Scene Tab)

| Property | Function |
|---|---|
| *Environment Lighting* | |
| Skybox | A skybox is an image that appears behind everything else in the scene so as to simulate the sky or other distant background. This property lets you choose the skybox asset you want to use for the scene. |
| Sun | When a procedural skybox is used, you can use this to specify a directional light object to indicate the direction of the "sun" (or whatever large, distant light source is illuminating your scene). If this is set to *None*, then the brightest directional light in the scene will be assumed to represent the sun. |
| Ambient Source | Ambient light is light that is present all around the scene and doesn't come from any specific source object. There are three options for the source of the ambient light. *Color* simply uses a flat color for all ambient light in the scene. *Gradient* lets you choose the color separately for ambient light from the sky, horizon, and ground, and blends smoothly between them. *Skybox* uses the colors of the skybox (if specified by the property described above) to determine the ambient light coming from different angles; this allows for more precise effects than the simpler Gradient option. |
| Ambient Intensity | The brightness of the ambient light in the scene. |
| Ambient GI | Specifies the GI mode (Precomputed Realtime or Baked) that should be used for handling the ambient light. This property has no effect unless both modes are enabled for the scene. |
| Reflection Source | Allows you to specify whether to use the skybox for reflection effects (the default) or alternatively choose a cubemap to use instead. If the skybox is selected as the source, then an additional option is provided to set the resolution of the skybox for reflection purposes. |
| Reflection Intensity | The degree to which the reflection source (skybox or cubemap) will be visible in reflective objects. |
| Reflection Bounces | A reflection "bounce" occurs where a reflection from one object is then reflected by another object. The reflections are captured in the scene through the use of <u>Reflection Probes</u>. This property lets you set how many times the bounces back and forth between objects are evaluated by the probes; if set to 1, then only the initial reflection (from the skybox or cubemap specified in the Reflection Source property) will be taken into account. |
| *Precomputed Real-Time GI* | |
| Realtime Resolution | This sets the number of texels (i.e., "texture pixels") that will be used per unit of length for objects being lit by realtime GI. A resolution of 1 per unit is usually a good value (depending on the size of the objects in the scene), but for terrains and huge objects, you will usually want to scale the resolution down. You can use the <u>Lightmap Parameters</u> or the <u>Mesh Renderer's</u> *Scale In Lightmap* property to reduce the resolution. Note that this property also sets the *Indirect Resolution* if both Realtime and Baked GI are enabled – see the *Baked GI* properties below. |

*(Continued)*

**(*Continued*)** Properties of Light Window (Scene Tab)

| Property | Function |
|---|---|
| CPU Usage | This lets you set the approximate amount of CPU time that should be spent evaluating realtime GI at runtime. Higher CPU usage results in faster reactions from the lighting but may affect frame rate. This does not affect the CPU usage for the precomputation process performed in the Editor. Note that higher CPU usage is achieved by increasing the number of threads assigned to the GI; processors with many cores may therefore suffer less of a performance hit. |
| *Baked GI* | |
| Baked Resolution | This sets the number of texels (i.e., "texture pixels") that will be used per unit of length for objects being lit by baked GI. This is typically set about ten times higher than the Realtime Resolution (see "Precomputed Realtime GI" above). |
| Baked Padding | The separation (in texel units) between separate shapes in the baked lightmap. |
| Compressed | Should the baked lightmap texture be compressed? A compressed lightmap requires less storage space, but the compression process can introduce unwanted artifacts into the texture. |
| Indirect Resolution | (Only available when Precomputed Realtime GI is disabled.) Resolution of the indirect lighting calculations. Equivalent to Realtime Resolution when using Precomputed Realtime GI. |
| Ambient Occlusion | The relative brightness of surfaces in ambient occlusion (i.e., partial blockage of ambient light in interior corners). Higher values indicate greater contrast between the occluded and fully lit areas. This is only applied to the indirect lighting calculated by the GI system. |
| Final Gather | When the final gather option is enabled, the final light bounce in the GI calculation will be calculated at the same resolution as the baked lightmap. This improves the visual quality of the lightmap but at the cost of additional baking time in the Editor. |
| *General GI* | |
| Directional Mode | The lightmap can be set up to store information about the dominant incoming light at each point on the objects' surfaces. In *Directional* mode, a second lightmap is generated to store the dominant direction of incoming light. This allows diffuse normal mapped materials to work with the GI. In *Directional Specular* mode, further data is stored to allow full shading incorporating specular reflection and normal maps. *Non-directional* mode switches both these options off. Directional mode requires about twice as much storage space for the additional lightmap data. Directional Specular requires four times as much storage and also about twice as much texture memory. |
| Indirect Intensity | A value that scales the brightness of indirect light as seen in the final lightmap (i.e., ambient light or light bounced and emitted from objects). Setting this to 1.0 uses the default scaling; values less than 1.0 reduce the intensity, while values greater than 1.0 increase it. |

*(Continued)*

**(*Continued*)** Properties of Light Window (Scene Tab)

| Property | Function |
| --- | --- |
| Bounce Boost | A scaling value to increase the amount of light bounced from surfaces onto other surfaces. The default value is 1.0 which indicates no increase. |
| Default Parameters | Unity™ uses a set of general parameters for the lightmapping in addition to properties of the Lighting window. A few defaults are available from the menu for this property, but you can also create your own Lightmap Parameter file using the Create New option. See the <u>Lightmap Parameters</u> page for further details. |
| Atlas Size | The size in pixels of the full lightmap texture which incorporates separate regions for the individual object textures. |
| *Fog* | |
| Fog Color | The color used to draw fog in the scene. Note that fog is not available with the <u>Deferred rendering path</u>. |
| Fog Mode | The way in which the fogging accumulates with distance from the camera. The options are *Linear*, *Exponential*, and *Exponential Squared* (these are in increasing order of fog accumulation with distance). |
| Start | (Only available for *Linear* fog mode) The distance from camera at which the fog starts. |
| End | (Only available for *Linear* fog mode) The distance from camera at which the fog completely obscures scene objects. |

## Properties of Rigidbody

| Property | Function |
| --- | --- |
| Mass | The mass of the object (in kilograms by default). |
| Drag | How much air resistance affects the object when moving from forces. 0 means no air resistance, and infinity makes the object stop moving immediately. |
| Angular Drag | How much air resistance affects the object when rotating from torque. 0 means no air resistance. Note that you cannot make the object stop rotating just by setting its Angular Drag to infinity. |
| Use Gravity | If enabled, the object is affected by gravity. |
| Is Kinematic | If enabled, the object will not be driven by the physics engine, and can only be manipulated by its Transform. This is useful for moving platforms or if you want to animate a Rigidbody that has a HingeJoint attached. |
| Interpolate | Try one of the options only if you are seeing jerkiness in your Rigidbody's movement. |
| • None | No Interpolation is applied. |
| • Interpolate | Transform is smoothed based on the Transform of the previous frame. |

(*Continued*)

**(*Continued*)** Properties of Rigidbody

| Property | Function |
|---|---|
| • Extrapolate | Transform is smoothed based on the estimated Transform of the next frame. |
| Collision Detection | Used to prevent fast moving objects from passing through other objects without detecting collisions. |
| • Discrete | Use Discrete collision detection against all other colliders in the scene. Other colliders will use Discrete collision detection when testing for collision against it. Used for normal collisions (this is the default value). |
| • Continuous | Use Discrete collision detection against dynamic colliders (with a rigidbody) and continuous collision detection against static MeshColliders (without a rigidbody). Rigidbodies set to Continuous Dynamic will use continuous collision detection when testing for collision against this rigidbody. Other rigidbodies will use Discrete Collision detection. Used for objects which the Continuous Dynamic detection needs to collide with. |
| • Continuous Dynamic | Use continuous collision detection against objects set to Continuous and Continuous Dynamic Collision. It will also use continuous collision detection against static MeshColliders (without a rigidbody). For all other colliders it uses discrete collision detection. Used for fast moving objects. |
| Constraints | Restrictions on the Rigidbody's motion:- |
| • Freeze Position | Stops the Rigidbody moving in the world X-, Y-, and Z-Axes selectively. |
| • Freeze Rotation | Stops the Rigidbody rotating around the world X-, Y-, and Z-Axes selectively. |

Properties of Light

| Property | Function |
|---|---|
| Type | The current type of light. Possible values are *Directional*, *Point*, *Spot*, and *Area* (see the <u>Lighting Overview</u> for details of these types). |
| Baking | This allows you to choose if the light should be baked if Baked GI is selected. Mixed will also bake it, but it will still be present at runtime to give direct lighting to non-static objects. Realtime works both for Precomputed Realtime GI and when not using GI. |
| Range | How far light is emitted from the center of the object (Point and Spotlights only). |
| Spot Angle | Determines the angle (in degrees) at the base of a spotlight's cone (Spotlight only). |
| Color | The color of the light emitted. |
| Intensity | Brightness of the light. The default value for a *Point*, *Spot*, or *Area* light is 1 but for a *Directional* light, it is 0.5. |

(*Continued*)

**(*Continued*) Properties of Light**

| Property | Function |
|---|---|
| Bounce Intensity | This allows you to vary the intensity of indirect light (i.e., light that is bounced from one object to another. The value is a multiple of the default brightness calculated by the GI system; if you set Bounce Intensity to a value greater than one, then bounced light will be made brighter, while a value less than one will make it dimmer. This is useful, for example, when a dark surface in shadow (such as the interior of a cave) needs to be rendered brighter in order to make detail visible. |
| Shadow Type | Determines whether *Hard Shadows Soft Shadows* or no shadows at all will be cast by this light. |
| Baked Shadow Radius | If shadows are enabled, then this property adds some artificial softening to the edges of shadows cast by point or spotlights. |
| Baked Shadow Angle | If shadows are enabled, then this property adds some artificial softening to the edges of shadows cast by directional lights. |
| Draw Halo | If checked, a spherical halo of light will be drawn with a radius equal to Range. |
| Flare | Optional reference to the Flare that will be rendered at the light's position. |
| Render Mode | Importance of this light. This can affect lighting fidelity and performance. The options are *Auto* (the rendering method is determined at runtime depending on the brightness of nearby lights and current Quality Settings), *Important* (the light is always rendered at per-pixel quality, and *Not Important* (the light is always rendered in a faster, vertex/object light mode). Use *Important* mode only for the most noticeable visual effects (e.g., headlights of a player's car). |
| Culling Mask | Use to selectively exclude groups of objects from being affected by the light (see Layers tab). |

**Properties of Camera**

| Property | Function |
|---|---|
| **Clear Flags** | Determine which parts of the screen will be cleared. This is handy when using multiple cameras to draw different game elements. |
| **Background** | The color applied to the remaining screen after all elements in view have been drawn and there is no skybox. |
| **Culling Mask** | Includes or omits layers of objects to be rendered by the camera. Assigns layers to your objects in the Inspector. |
| **Projection** | Toggles the camera's capability to simulate perspective. |
| *Perspective* | Camera will render objects with perspective intact. |
| *Orthographic* | Camera will render objects uniformly, with no sense of perspective. |
| **Size** (Orthographic) | The viewport size of the camera when set to Orthographic. |
| **Field of view** (Perspective) | The width of the camera's view angle, measured in degrees along the local Y-Axis. |

*(Continued)*

(*Continued*) Properties of Camera

| Property | Function |
| --- | --- |
| **Clipping Planes** | Distances from the camera to start and stop rendering. |
| *Near* | The closest point relative to the camera that drawing will occur. |
| *Far* | The furthest point relative to the camera that drawing will occur. |
| **Normalized Viewport Rect** | Four values that indicate where on the screen, this camera view will be drawn. Measured in Screen Coordinates (values 0–1). |
| *X* | The beginning horizontal position that the camera view will be drawn. |
| *Y* | The beginning vertical position that the camera view will be drawn. |
| *W* (Width) | Width of the camera output on the screen. |
| *H* (Height) | Height of the camera output on the screen. |
| **Depth** | The camera's position in the draw order. Cameras with a larger value will be drawn on top of cameras with a smaller value. |
| **Rendering Path** | Options for defining what rendering methods will be used by the camera. |
| *Use Player Settings* | This camera will use whichever Rendering Path is set in the Player Settings. |
| *Vertex Lit* | All objects rendered by this camera will be rendered as Vertex-Lit objects. |
| *Forward* | All objects will be rendered with one pass per material. |
| *Deferred Lighting* | All objects will be drawn once without lighting; then lighting of all objects will be rendered together at the end of the render queue. |
| **Target Texture** | Reference to a <u>Render Texture</u> that will contain the output of the Camera view. Setting this reference will disable this Camera's capability to render to the screen. |
| **HDR** | Enables High Dynamic Range rendering for this camera. |
| **Target Display** | Defines which external device to render to. Between 1 and 8. |

# Appendix C: Joystick Software Installation

To link the key controls to the Logitech Extreme 3D Pro Joystick Controller, first download the Logitech Profiler for the joystick controller from the Logitech support website: https://support.logi.com/hc/en-us/ articles/360024843033--Downloads-Extreme-3D-Pro. As shown in Figure C1, select the Windows OS you are using and whether your computer is a 32-bit or 64-bit before clicking the Download button. Once downloaded, run your Logitech Profiler setup as shown in Figure C2. Select your language and click on Next as shown in Figure C3.

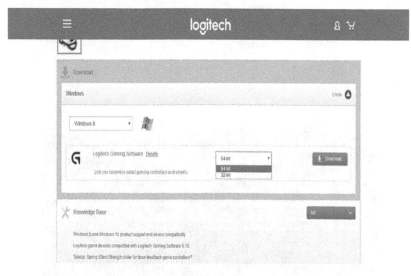

**FIGURE C1**
Logitech support website.

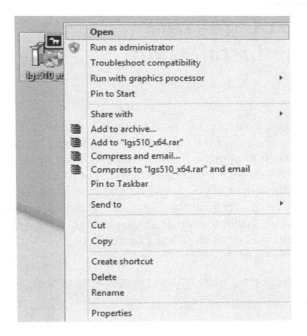

**FIGURE C2**
Running the setup.

**FIGURE C3**
Selecting your language.

Then select "I accept the terms in the license agreement", and click Install as shown in Figure C4. Wait for the setup to finish the installation; then select Done as shown in Figure C5.

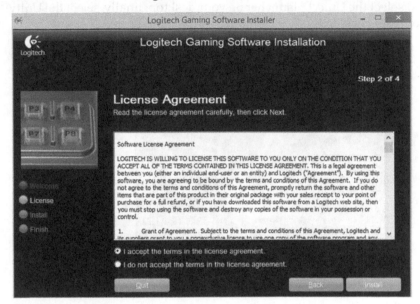

**FIGURE C4**
Accept the terms of agreement.

**FIGURE C5**
Finished setup.

Having downloaded the Logitech Profiler, connect your joystick controller before opening your profiler from the desktop (Figure C6). In the Logitech Profiler, click on Profile > new. Give the profile a name; then click Browse and select the Unity™ launcher on your desktop; finally, select the Unity™ icon, and click on the "OK" button as shown in Figure C7.

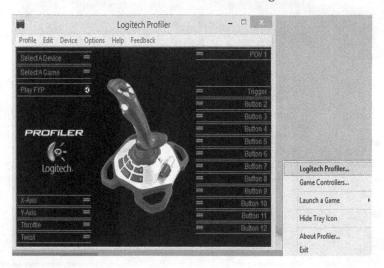

**FIGURE C6**
Opening Logitech Profiler.

**FIGURE C7**
Create new profile.

Next, click on X-Axis > select zone assignment > new zone assignment as shown in Figure C8. In the zone assignment window, name your X-Axis; then press the Split button once; then arrange the split segments into the configuration as shown in Figure C9.

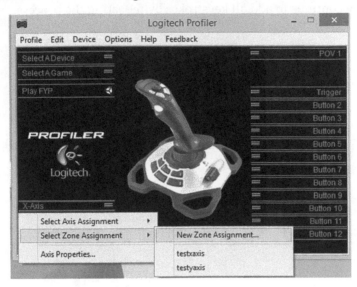

**FIGURE C8**
Setting the X-Axis.

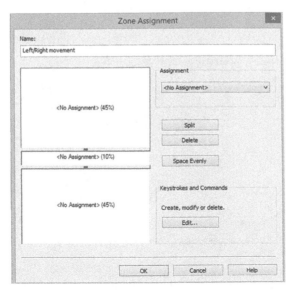

**FIGURE C9**
New zone assignment.

Next click on the Edit button shown in Figure C10, and add the keystrokes assigned to the keyboard by click on new keystroke. Click the Record button and then press the key you wish to record followed by the stop Button in Figure C11. Each new keystroke can only record one key at a time, but you may continue to add all keystrokes by repeating the process.

**FIGURE C10**
New keystroke.

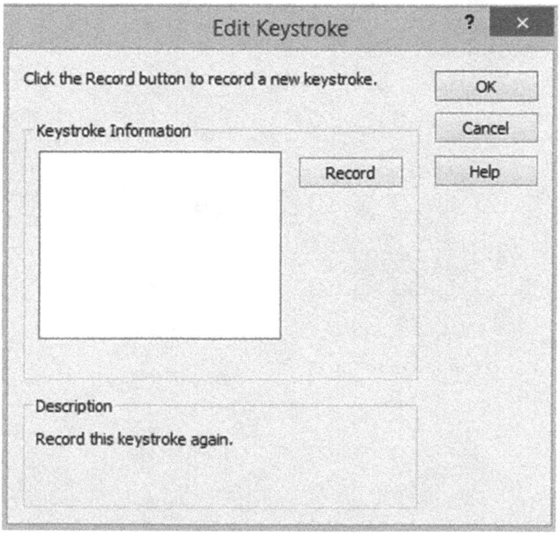

**FIGURE C11**
Recording a key.

**FIGURE C12**
Recording "A" button.

Once all keystrokes have been recorded, assign the keys for your axis in the zone assignment window shown earlier in Figure C12. Select the top portion; then click the drop-down list, and select "keystroke A" in Figure C13; repeat for the bottom portion with "keystroke D" as shown in Figure C14. Leave the middle portion blank so that the ROV will no sway at rest.

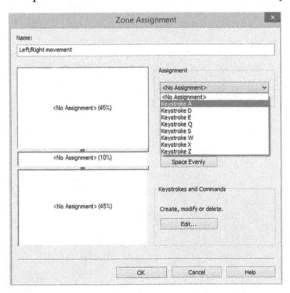

**FIGURE C13**
Assign keystroke "A".

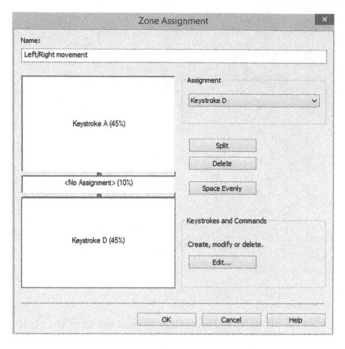

**FIGURE C14**
Assign keystroke "D".

# Appendix D: Scripts

## Grid.cs

```csharp
using UnityEngine;
using System.Collections;
using System.Collections.Generic;

public class Grid : MonoBehaviour {
    public bool displayGridGizmos;
    public Transform player;
    public LayerMask unwalkableMask;          // Member Variables
    public Vector2 gridWorldSize;
    public float nodeRadius;
    Node[,] grid;
                                              // Initializing size of grid to be created
    float nodeDiameter;
    int gridSizeX, gridSizeY;

    void Awake() {
        nodeDiameter = nodeRadius * 2;
        gridSizeX = Mathf.RoundToInt (gridWorldSize.x / nodeDiameter);
        gridSizeY = Mathf.RoundToInt (gridWorldSize.y / nodeDiameter);
        CreateGrid ();
    }                                         // Get the function
                                              // that returns the max
    public int MaxSize {                      // number the cells of
        get {                                 // 2D grid
            return gridSizeX * gridSizeY;
        }
    }

    void CreateGrid() {
        grid = new Node[gridSizeX, gridSizeY];
        Vector3 worldBottomLeft = transform.position - Vector3.right * gridWorldSize.x / 2
            - Vector3.forward * gridWorldSize.y / 2;
        for (int x = 0; x < gridSizeX; x ++) {
            for (int y = 0; y < gridSizeY; y ++) {
                Vector3 worldPoint = worldBottomLeft + Vector3.right * (x * nodeDiameter + nodeRadius)
                    + Vector3.forward * (y * nodeDiameter + nodeRadius);
                bool walkable = !(Physics.CheckSphere (worldPoint, nodeRadius,unwalkableMask));
                grid [x, y] = new Node (walkable, worldPoint, x,y);
            }
        }
    }

    public List<Node> GetNeighbours(Node node) {
        List<Node> neighbours = new List<Node> ();

        for (int x = -1; x <= 1; x++) {
            for (int y = -1; y <= 1; y++) {
                if (x == 0 && y == 0)
                    continue;

                int checkX = node.gridX + x;
                int checkY = node.gridY + y;

                if (checkX >= 0 && checkX < gridSizeX && checkY >= 0 && checkY < gridSizeY) {
                    neighbours.Add (grid [checkX, checkY]);
                }
            }
        }

        return neighbours;
```

```
public Node NodeFromWorldPoint(Vector3 worldPosition) {
    float percentX = (worldPosition.x + gridWorldSize.x / 2) / gridWorldSize.x;
    float percentY = (worldPosition.z + gridWorldSize.y / 2) / gridWorldSize.y;
    percentX = Mathf.Clamp01 (percentX);
    percentY = Mathf.Clamp01 (percentY);

    int x = Mathf.RoundToInt((gridSizeX - 1) * percentX);
        int y = Mathf.RoundToInt((gridSizeY - 1) * percentY);
    return grid [x, y];
}

void OnDrawGizmos () {
    Gizmos.DrawWireCube (transform.position, new Vector3 (gridWorldSize.x, 1, gridWorldSize.y));
    if (grid != null && displayGridGizmos) {
        foreach (Node n in grid) {
            Gizmos.color = (n.walkable) ? Color.white : Color.red;
            Gizmos.DrawCube (n.worldPosition, Vector3.one * (nodeDiameter - .1f));
        }
    }
}
}
```

# Heap.cs

```csharp
using UnityEngine;
using System.Collections;
using System;

public class Heap<T> where T : IHeapItem<T> {
    T[] items;
    int currentItemCount;

    public Heap (int maxHeapSize) {
        items = new T[maxHeapSize];
    }

    public void Add(T item) {
        item.HeapIndex = currentItemCount;
        items [currentItemCount] = item;
        SortUp (item);
        currentItemCount++;
    }

    public T RemoveFirst() {
        T firstItem = items [0];
        currentItemCount--;
        items [0] = items [currentItemCount];
        items [0].HeapIndex = 0;
        SortDown (items [0]);
        return firstItem;
    }

    public void UpdateItem(T item) {
        SortUp (item);
    }

    public int Count {
        get {
            return currentItemCount;
        }
    }

    public bool Contains(T item) {
        return Equals (items [item.HeapIndex], item);
    }

    void SortDown(T item) {
        while (true) {
            int childIndexLeft = item.HeapIndex * 2 + 1;
            int childIndexRight = item.HeapIndex * 2 + 2;
            int swapIndex = 0;

            if (childIndexLeft < currentItemCount) {
                swapIndex = childIndexLeft;

                if (childIndexRight < currentItemCount) {
                    if (items[childIndexLeft].CompareTo(items[childIndexRight]) < 0) {
                        swapIndex = childIndexRight;
                    }
                }

                if (item.CompareTo(items[swapIndex]) < 0) {
                    Swap (item,items[swapIndex]);
                }
                else{
                    return;
                }
            }
            else {
                return;
            }
        }
```

```
void SortUp(T item) {
    int parentIndex = (item.HeapIndex - 1) / 2;

    while (true) {
        T parentItem = items [parentIndex];
        if (item.CompareTo (parentItem) > 0) {
            Swap (item, parentItem);
        }
        else {
            break;
        }

        parentIndex = (item.HeapIndex - 1) / 2;
    }
}

void Swap(T itemA, T itemB) {
    items [itemA.HeapIndex] = itemB;
    items [itemB.HeapIndex] = itemA;
    int itemAIndex = itemA.HeapIndex;
    itemA.HeapIndex = itemB.HeapIndex;
    itemB.HeapIndex = itemAIndex;
}

}

public interface IHeapItem<T> : IComparable<T> {
    int HeapIndex {
        get;
        set;
    }
}
```

## Node.cs

```
using UnityEngine;
using System.Collections;

public class Node : IHeapItem<Node> {

    public bool walkable;
    public Vector3 worldPosition;
    public int gridX;
    public int gridY;

    public int gCost;
    public int hCost;
    public Node parent;
    int heapIndex;

    public Node(bool _walkable, Vector3 _worldPos, int _gridX, int _gridY) {
        walkable = _walkable;
        worldPosition = _worldPos;
        gridX = _gridX;
        gridY = _gridY;
    }

    public int fCost {
        get {
            return gCost + hCost;
        }
    }

    public int HeapIndex {
        get {
            return heapIndex;
        }
        set {
            heapIndex = value;
        }
    }

    public int CompareTo(Node nodeToCompare) {
        int compare = fCost.CompareTo (nodeToCompare.fCost);
        if (compare == 0) {
            compare = hCost.CompareTo (nodeToCompare.hCost);
        }
        return -compare;
    }
}
```

This script stores information for the A* node, similar to heap.cs.

## ROVCamera.cs

```
using System.Collections;
using System.Collections.Generic;
using UnityEngine;

public class ROVCamera : MonoBehaviour {

    public List<GameObject> Cameras;
    int CameraListIndex;

    void Start () {
        CameraListIndex = 0;
    }

    void Update () {
        if(Input.GetKeyUp(KeyCode.C))
        {
            Cameras[CameraListIndex++].SetActive(false);

            CameraListIndex = CameraListIndex == Cameras.Count ? 0 : CameraListIndex;

            Cameras[CameraListIndex].SetActive(true);
        }
    }
}
```

Annotations:
- List the cameras
- Start View from 1st Camera
- Set current cam unactive
- Set next cam active

This script enables toggling between cameras to look at the ROV from different views in the games.

# Pathfinding.cs

```csharp
using UnityEngine;
using System.Collections;
using System.Collections.Generic;
using System.Diagnostics;
using System;

public class Pathfinding : MonoBehaviour {

    PathRequestManager requestManager;
    Grid grid;

    void Awake() {
        requestManager = GetComponent<PathRequestManager> ();
        grid = GetComponent<Grid> ();
    }

    public void StartFindPath(Vector3 startPos, Vector3 targetPos) {
        StartCoroutine (FindPath (startPos, targetPos));
    }

    IEnumerator FindPath(Vector3 startPos, Vector3 targetPos) {

        Stopwatch sw = new Stopwatch ();
        sw.Start ();

        Vector3[] waypoints = new Vector3[0];
        bool pathSuccess = false;

        Node startNode = grid.NodeFromWorldPoint (startPos);
        Node targetNode = grid.NodeFromWorldPoint (targetPos);

        if (startNode.walkable && targetNode.walkable) {
            Heap<Node> openSet = new Heap<Node> (grid.MaxSize);
            HashSet<Node> closedSet = new HashSet<Node> ();
            openSet.Add (startNode);

            while (openSet.Count > 0) {
                Node currentNode = openSet.RemoveFirst ();
                closedSet.Add (currentNode);

                if (currentNode == targetNode) {
                    sw.Stop ();
                    print ("Path found: " + sw.ElapsedMilliseconds + "ms");
                    pathSuccess = true;
                    break;
                }

                foreach (Node neighbour in grid.GetNeighbours(currentNode)) {
                    if (!neighbour.walkable || closedSet.Contains (neighbour)) {
                        continue;
                    }

                    int newMovementCostToNeighbour = currentNode.gCost + Getdistance (currentNode, neighbour);
                    if (newMovementCostToNeighbour < neighbour.gCost || !openSet.Contains (neighbour)) {
                        neighbour.gCost = newMovementCostToNeighbour;
                        neighbour.hCost = Getdistance (neighbour, targetNode);
                        neighbour.parent = currentNode;

                        if (!openSet.Contains (neighbour))
                            openSet.Add (neighbour);
                        else {
                            openSet.UpdateItem (neighbour);
                        }
                    }
                }
            }
        }
```

```
        yield return null;
        if (pathSuccess) {
            waypoints = RetracePath (startNode, targetNode);
        }
        requestManager.FinishedProcessingPath (waypoints, pathSuccess);
    }

}

Vector3[] RetracePath (Node startNode, Node endNode) {
    List<Node> path = new List<Node> ();
    Node currentNode = endNode;

    while (currentNode != startNode) {
        path.Add (currentNode);
        currentNode = currentNode.parent;
    }
    Vector3[] waypoints = SimplifyPath (path);
    Array.Reverse(waypoints);
    return waypoints;

}

Vector3[] SimplifyPath(List<Node> path){
    List<Vector3> waypoints = new List<Vector3> ();
    Vector2 directionOld = Vector2.zero;

    for (int i = 1; i < path.Count; i++) {
        Vector2 directionNew = new Vector2 (path [i - 1].gridX - path [i].gridX, path [i - 1].gridY - path [i].gridY);
        if (directionNew != directionOld) {
            waypoints.Add (path [i].worldPosition);
        }
        directionOld = directionNew;
    }
    return waypoints.ToArray ();
}

int Getdistance(Node nodeA, Node nodeB) {
    int dstX = Mathf.Abs (nodeA.gridX - nodeB.gridX);
    int dstY = Mathf.Abs (nodeA.gridY - nodeB.gridY);

    if (dstX > dstY)
        return 14 * dstY + 10 * (dstX - dstY);
    return 14 * dstX + 10 * (dstY - dstX);
}
}
```

Use multiple threads to make the process faster

Changing Data Structure

This script checks whether the start and end points are in positions and finds the shortest path between them.

## PathRequestManager.cs

```
using UnityEngine;
using System.Collections;
using System.Collections.Generic;
using System;

public class PathRequestManager : MonoBehaviour {
    Queue<PathRequest> pathRequestQueue = new Queue<PathRequest>();
    PathRequest currentPathRequest;

    static PathRequestManager instance;
    Pathfinding pathfinding;

    bool isProcessingPath;

    void Awake() {
        instance = this;
        pathfinding = GetComponent<Pathfinding>();
    }

    public static void RequestPath(Vector3 pathStart, Vector3 pathEnd, Action<Vector3[], bool> callback) {
        PathRequest newRequest = new PathRequest(pathStart,pathEnd,callback);
        instance.pathRequestQueue.Enqueue(newRequest);
        instance.TryProcessNext();
    }

    void TryProcessNext() {
        if (!isProcessingPath && pathRequestQueue.Count > 0) {
            currentPathRequest = pathRequestQueue.Dequeue();
            isProcessingPath = true;
            pathfinding.StartFindPath(currentPathRequest.pathStart, currentPathRequest.pathEnd);
        }
    }

    public void FinishedProcessingPath(Vector3[] path, bool success) {
        currentPathRequest.callback(path,success);
        isProcessingPath = false;
        TryProcessNext();
    }

    struct PathRequest {
        public Vector3 pathStart;
        public Vector3 pathEnd;
        public Action<Vector3[], bool> callback;

        public PathRequest(Vector3 _start, Vector3 _end, Action<Vector3[], bool> _callback) {
            pathStart = _start;
            pathEnd = _end;
            callback = _callback;
        }

    }
}
```

Initialize a new queue to set the waypoints

At the start of the program

Complete finish the waypoint

This script initializes the path to be taken by the ROV and stores the waypoints to the destination.

## Underwater.cs

```
using UnityEngine;
using System.Collections;

public class underwater : MonoBehaviour
{
    public int underwaterLevel = 7;
    public float varFogDensity = 0.0f;        } Define Variable

    private bool defaultFog;
    private Color defaultFogColor;
    private float defaultFogDensity;           } The scene's
    private Material defaultSkybox;               default fog settings
    private Material noSkybox = null;
    public GameObject cameraObj;

    void Start()
    {
        defaultFog = RenderSettings.fog;
        defaultFogColor = RenderSettings.fogColor;
        defaultFogDensity = RenderSettings.fogDensity;
        defaultSkybox = RenderSettings.skybox;

        Camera camera = cameraObj.GetComponent<Camera>();

        if (camera)                                            } Set
        {                                                         background
            camera.backgroundColor = new Color(0, 0.4f, 0.7f, 1);   color
        }
    }

    void Update()
    {
        if (transform.position.y < underwaterLevel)
        {
            RenderSettings.fog = true;
            RenderSettings.fogColor = new Color(0, 0.4f, 0.7f, 0.6f);
            RenderSettings.fogDensity = varFogDensity;
            RenderSettings.skybox = noSkybox;
        }
        else
        {
            RenderSettings.fog = defaultFog;
            RenderSettings.fogColor = defaultFogColor;
            RenderSettings.fogDensity = defaultFogDensity;
            RenderSettings.skybox = defaultSkybox;
        }
    }
}
```

This script generates the underwater fog effect seen in the simulation.

# Playerinput.cs

```csharp
using UnityEngine;
using System.Collections;
using System.Collections.Generic;

public class PlayerInput : MonoBehaviour {

    public struct Position
    {
        public Vector3 forwardAmount;
        public float turnAmount;
    }

    public Transform ROV;
    public float moveSpeed = 0.0f;
    public float rotationSpeed = 0.0f;
    public bool isActivateArm = false;
    public bool isAuto = false;
    public bool isInput = false;
    public GameObject Spotlight;
    bool isOnSpotLight = true;

    [Range(0.01f, 1.0f)]
    public float shipSmoothness = 0.5f;

    Vector3 moveVector;

    public Position m_position, m_target;
    public Vector3 m_speed;

    const float MAX_ACCELERATION = 1.0f;

    public float DECELERATION_RATE = 0.25f;

    float m_acceleration = 0.0f;

    Vector3 m_previousPos, m_velocity;

    void Start () {
        m_target = m_position;

        m_previousPos = ROV.transform.position;
    }

    void LateUpdate ()
    {
        ProcessInput();

        InterpolateToTarget();

        MoveShip();
    }
```

Set the starting position to itself → Initialization of ROV positioning

Update is called once per frame

```
void ProcessInput()
{
    float speed = moveSpeed;
    float velocity = m_velocity.magnitude;

    m_target.forwardAmount = Vector3.zero;
    m_target.turnAmount = 0.0f;

    isInput = false;

    if (!isAuto)
    {
        if (Input.GetKey(KeyCode.A))
        {
            m_acceleration += Time.deltaTime;

            moveVector = -ROV.right;

            isInput = true;
        }
        if (Input.GetKey(KeyCode.D))
        {
            m_acceleration += Time.deltaTime;

            moveVector = ROV.right;

            isInput = true;
        }

        if (Input.GetKey(KeyCode.W))
        {
            m_acceleration += Time.deltaTime;

            moveVector = ROV.forward;

            isInput = true;
        }
        if (Input.GetKey(KeyCode.S))
        {
            m_acceleration += Time.deltaTime;

            moveVector = -ROV.forward;

            isInput = true;
        }
        if (Input.GetKey(KeyCode.Q))
        {
            ROV.transform.Rotate(Vector3.up, -Time.deltaTime * rotationSpeed);
        }
        if (Input.GetKey(KeyCode.E))
        {
            ROV.transform.Rotate(Vector3.up, Time.deltaTime * rotationSpeed);
        }
```

Reset the values

Move Right

Move Left

Move Forward

Move Backward

Yaw Right

Yaw Left

```
if (Input.GetKey(KeyCode.I))
{
    ROV.transform.Rotate(Vector3.right, -Time.deltaTime * rotationSpeed);
}
if (Input.GetKey(KeyCode.K))
{
    ROV.transform.Rotate(Vector3.right, Time.deltaTime * rotationSpeed);
}
if (Input.GetKey(KeyCode.L))
{
    ROV.transform.Rotate(Vector3.forward, -Time.deltaTime * rotationSpeed);
}
if (Input.GetKey(KeyCode.J))
{
    ROV.transform.Rotate(Vector3.forward, Time.deltaTime * rotationSpeed);
}
if (Input.GetKey(KeyCode.Z))
{
    m_acceleration += Time.deltaTime;

    moveVector = -ROV.up;

    isInput = true;
}
if (Input.GetKey(KeyCode.X) && transform.position.y < 15.0f)
{
    m_acceleration += Time.deltaTime;

    moveVector = ROV.up;

    isInput = true;
}
if (Input.GetKeyUp(KeyCode.Tab))
{
    isActivateArm = !isActivateArm;
}
if (Input.GetKeyUp(KeyCode.F))
{
    isOnSpotLight = !isOnSpotLight;
    Spotlight.SetActive(isOnSpotLight);
}

m_acceleration = Mathf.Clamp(m_acceleration, 0.0f, MAX_ACCELERATION);

moveVector.Normalize();

m_target.forwardAmount += moveVector * speed * m_acceleration * Time.deltaTime;

float dt = Time.deltaTime * 1000.0f;
float amount = Mathf.Pow(1.02f, Mathf.Min(dt, 1.0f));
```

Pitch Forward

Pitch Backward

Roll Right

Roll Left

Move Downward

Move Upward with a limit to the ROV's maximum height, to prevent leaving simulated area

Activate Arms

Activate Light

```
            if (!isInput)
            {
                m_acceleration -= Time.deltaTime * DECELERATION_RATE;
            }
        }
    }
    void InterpolateToTarget()
    {
        if (Time.timeScale == 0.0f)
        {
            m_position = m_target;
            return;
        }
        float smoothness;

        smoothness = 1.0f / Mathf.Clamp(shipSmoothness, 0.01f, 1.0f);
        float shipLerp = Mathf.Clamp01(Time.deltaTime * smoothness);

        m_position.forwardAmount = Vector3.Lerp(m_position.forwardAmount, m_target.forwardAmount, shipLerp);
        m_position.turnAmount = Mathf.Lerp(m_position.turnAmount, m_target.turnAmount, shipLerp);

        m_speed = m_position.forwardAmount / Time.deltaTime;
    }

    void MoveShip()
    {
        ROV.transform.position += m_position.forwardAmount;

        m_velocity = ROV.transform.position - m_previousPos;
        m_previousPos = ROV.transform.position;

    }
}
```

> Move the ROV accordingly during manual

> If time is zero, don't move

> Move the ROV

This script updates (moves) the positioning and direction of the ROV when keys are clicked.

# Unit.cs

```
using UnityEngine;
using System.Collections;
using System.Collections.Generic;

public class Unit : MonoBehaviour {
    public List<Transform> waypoints;
    int waypointindex = 0;

    public bool isLoop = false;
    public bool isAuto = true;
    public bool isLeak = false;
    bool moveObj = true;
    bool rotateObj = false;
    public float speed = 5;
    Vector3[] path;
    int targetIndex;
    bool isPlaneFloor = false;

    void Start()
    {
    }

    public void OnPathFound(Vector3[] newPath, bool pathSuccessful) {
        if (pathSuccessful) {
            path = newPath;
            targetIndex = 0;
            StopCoroutine("FollowPath");
            StartCoroutine("FollowPath");
        }
    }

    void Update()
    {
        if (isAuto)
        {
            if (!isPlaneFloor)
            {
                if ((transform.position.y < 5.9 || transform.position.y > 6.1))
                {
                    float newY = transform.position.y;
                    float difference = transform.position.y < 6.0f ? 1.0f : -1.0f;
                    newY += difference * 2.0f * Time.deltaTime;
                    transform.position = new Vector3(transform.position.x, newY, transform.position.z);

                }
                else
                {
                    PathRequestManager.RequestPath(transform.position, waypoints[waypointindex].position, OnPathFound);

                    isPlaneFloor = true;
                }
            }
        }
```

List waypoints in unity

Number of waypoints, default=0

Member Variables

Start to move along the path if there is a successful path

During Auto Move

Move to a certain height to use the AI pathfinding

```
        if (Input.GetKeyUp(KeyCode.R) && !isAuto)
        {
            waypointindex = 0;

            PlayerInput m_pi = GetComponent<PlayerInput>();
            if(m_pi)
            {
                m_pi.isAuto = true;
            }

            isAuto = true;
            isPlaneFloor = false;
            moveObj = false;
            rotateObj = true;
        }
    }

    IEnumerator FollowPath()
    {
        if(path[0] == null || isLeak)
        {
            yield break;
        }

        Vector3 currentTargetPoint = path[0];
        while (true)
        {
            if ((Input.GetKeyUp(KeyCode.R) && isAuto))
            {
                isAuto = false;
                PlayerInput m_pi = GetComponent<PlayerInput>();
                if (m_pi)
                {
                    m_pi.isAuto = false;
                }

                yield break;
            }

            if (moveObj)
            {
                speed = 5.0f;

                if (transform.position == currentTargetPoint)
                {
                    moveObj = false;
                    rotateObj = true;
                    ++targetIndex;

                    if (targetIndex > path.Length - 1)
                    {
                        targetIndex = 0;

                        if (isLoop)
                        {
                            waypointindex = (++waypointindex < waypoints.Count) ? waypointindex : 0;
                            PathRequestManager.RequestPath(transform.position, waypoints[waypointindex].position, OnPathFound);
                        }
```

Check if R button has been pressed, set as restart button

If no path or ROV founds leak

Change to manual when key pressed

Go to next target point

Check if obj at target point

Reset target index

If at end of target point list, get new list of target point

```
                        else
                        {
                            if (++waypointindex < waypoints.Count)
                            {
                                PathRequestManager.RequestPath(transform.position, waypoints[waypointindex].position, OnPathFound);
                            }
                            else
                            {
                                yield break;
                            }
                        }

                    }

                    currentTargetPoint = path[targetIndex];
                }
                transform.position = Vector3.MoveTowards(transform.position, currentTargetPoint, speed * Time.deltaTime);
            }
        if(rotateObj)
        {
            speed = 0.0f;

            Vector3 newTargetDir = path[targetIndex] - transform.position;
            float angleinRadians = Mathf.Acos(Vector3.Dot(transform.forward.normalized, newTargetDir.normalized));
            float angleinDegrees = angleinRadians * 57.2958f;

            if(angleinDegrees > 2.0f)
            {
                float angle = 10.0f * Time.deltaTime;
                float direction = (Vector3.Dot(transform.right.normalized, newTargetDir.normalized) < 0) ? -1 : 1;
                transform.eulerAngles = new Vector3(transform.eulerAngles.x, transform.eulerAngles.y + angle * direction, transform.eulerAngles.z);
            }
            else
            {
                moveObj = true;
                rotateObj = false;
            }
        }

        yield return null;
```
⟶ Yield return null required in loop to run at correct speed

```
    }
    public void OnDrawGizmos() {
        if (path != null) {
            for (int i = targetIndex; i < path.Length; i ++) {
                Gizmos.color = Color.black;
                Gizmos.DrawCube(path[i], Vector3.one);

                if (i == targetIndex) {
                    Gizmos.DrawLine(transform.position, path[i]);
                }
                else {
                    Gizmos.DrawLine(path[i-1],path[i]);
                }
            }
        }
    }
}
```

Draw the debug lines, used to show path (used in the beginning only)

This script controls the movement of the simulated ROV.

## UIPlay.cs

```
using System.Collections;
using System.Collections.Generic;
using UnityEngine;
using UnityEngine.UI;
using UnityEngine.SceneManagement;

public class UIPlay : MonoBehaviour {

    void Start () {
        Button btn = GetComponent<Button>();

        if (btn)
        {
            btn.onClick.AddListener(TaskOnClick);
        }
    }

    void TaskOnClick()
    {
        SceneManager.LoadScene("pathfinding", LoadSceneMode.Single);
    }
}
```

Main Menu Play Button

On click, load the scene pathfinding

This script enables the "play" button in the TitleScreen scene, switching to the pathfinding scene when clicked.

## UImainmenu.cs

```
using System.Collections;
using System.Collections.Generic;
using UnityEngine;
using UnityEngine.UI;
using UnityEngine.SceneManagement;

public class UImainmenu : MonoBehaviour
{
    void Start()
    {
        Button btn = GetComponent<Button>();

        if (btn)
        {
            btn.onClick.AddListener(TaskOnClick);
        }
    }

    void TaskOnClick()
    {
        SceneManager.LoadScene("TitleScreen", LoadSceneMode.Single);
    }
}
```

Use this for initialization

On click load the scene TitleScreen

This script enables the "back to main menu" button in the pathfinding scene, switching to the TitleScreen when clicked.

# ROVcollision.cs

```csharp
using System.Collections;
using System.Collections.Generic;
using UnityEngine;

public class ROVcollision : MonoBehaviour
{

    public GameObject EmergencyLight;
    public GameObject Leak;

    void Start()
    {

    }

    void Update()
    {
    }

    void OnCollisionEnter(Collision collision)
    {
        Unit m_unit = null;
        PlayerInput m_playerinput = null;

        m_unit = GetComponent<Unit>();
        m_playerinput = GetComponent<PlayerInput>();

        if (m_unit && m_playerinput)
        {
            if (collision.gameObject.name == "5-leak")
            {
                m_unit.isLeak = true;
                EmergencyLight.SetActive(true);

            }
            if (collision.gameObject.name == "shutdownbutton" && m_unit.isLeak && m_playerinput.isActivateArm)
            {
                EmergencyLight.SetActive(false);
                m_unit.isLeak = false;
                Leak.SetActive(false);
            }
        }
    }

    void OnCollisionExit(Collision collision)
    {

    }
}
```

When ROV senses the leak, turn on emergency light

This script governs the sensing of the leak and collision with the Shutdown button.

## ROVARM.cs

```csharp
using System.Collections;
using System.Collections.Generic;
using UnityEngine;

public class ROVARM : MonoBehaviour {

    public GameObject ROV;
    PlayerInput ROV_PI;          // Variables Used

    public GameObject leftArm;
    public GameObject rightArm;
    public float rotateFactor = 1.0f;

    void Start ()
    {
        ROV_PI = ROV.GetComponent<PlayerInput>();
    }

    void Update ()
    {
        if (ROV_PI)
        {
            if (ROV_PI.isActivateArm)
            {
                if (rightArm.transform.localEulerAngles.y <= 90.0f)
                {
                    rightArm.transform.Rotate(Vector3.up, rotateFactor * Time.deltaTime);
                }
                if (leftArm.transform.localEulerAngles.y >= 270.0f)
                {
                    leftArm.transform.Rotate(Vector3.up, -rotateFactor * Time.deltaTime);
                }
            }

            else
            {
                if (rightArm.transform.localEulerAngles.y > 1.0f)
                {
                    rightArm.transform.Rotate(Vector3.up, -rotateFactor * Time.deltaTime);
                }
                if (leftArm.transform.localEulerAngles.y <= 350.0f)
                {
                    leftArm.transform.Rotate(Vector3.up, rotateFactor * Time.deltaTime);
                }
            }
        }
    }
}
```

Labels in left margin: "Arm Open" and "Arm Close"

This script controls the activation of the arm manipulators on the ROV.

## PropellerMove.cs

```
using System.Collections;
using System.Collections.Generic;
using UnityEngine;

public class PropellerMove : MonoBehaviour {

    public GameObject leftPropeller;
    public GameObject rightPropeller;
    public float speed = 100;

    void Start () {

    }

    void Update () {
        leftPropeller.transform.Rotate(Vector3.forward, speed * Time.deltaTime);
        rightPropeller.transform.Rotate(Vector3.forward, speed * Time.deltaTime);
    }
}
```

Rotate propellers
(Left and Right)

This script governs the rotation of the ROVs propellers.

## EmergencyLight.cs

```csharp
using System.Collections;
using System.Collections.Generic;
using UnityEngine;

public class EmergencyLight : MonoBehaviour {

    Light m_light;
    bool isIncreasing = false;
    public float intensitySpeed = 1.0f;
    public float maxintensity = 1.0f;

    void Start () {
        m_light = GetComponent<Light>();
    }

    void Update () {
        if(m_light)
        {
            if(isIncreasing)
            {
                m_light.intensity += intensitySpeed * Time.deltaTime;

                if (m_light.intensity >= maxintensity)
                {
                    isIncreasing = false;
                }
            }
            else
            {
                m_light.intensity -= intensitySpeed * Time.deltaTime;

                if (m_light.intensity <= 0.01f)
                {
                    isIncreasing = true;
                }
            }
        }
    }
}
```

Light will flash, by changing intensity from zero to max and vice versa

This script controls the flashing of the emergency light.

# CanvasScript.cs

```
void Update ()
{
    m_latlongtext.text = "Lat, Long: " + ROV.transform.position.x.ToString("G4") + ", " + ROV.transform.position.z.ToString("G4");

    m_depthtext.text = "Depth: " + (900.0f - ROV.transform.position.y).ToString("G4");        ⟶ [Depth]

    m_headingtext.text = "Heading: " + (ROV.transform.eulerAngles.y).ToString("G4");          ⟶ [Heading]

    if (ROV_autovelocity.isAuto)
    {
        m_speedtext.text = "Speed: " + ROV_autovelocity.speed;          } [Speed when auto]
    }
    else
    {
        m_speedtext.text = "Speed: " + ROV_manualvelocity.m_speed.magnitude.ToString("G4");          } [Speed when manual]
    }

    curTime += Time.deltaTime;

    m_runtimetext.text = "Time Elapsed: " + curTime.ToString("G3");          ⟶ [Run Time]
}
```

This script controls the text displays shown in the scene.

# Index

Note: **Bold** page numbers refer to tables; *italic* page numbers refer to figures.

ANOVA test, one-way 89, **90**
assets, import 3D models into *29*
Awake() functions 65

ButtonScript 76–78, *77–79*

camera
    properties of 102–103
    settings for remotely operated
        vehicle (ROV) **49**, *50*
$CO_3$-AUVs 3
CryEngine 6

DeepWorks ROV **2**
Det Norske Veritas (DNV) standard 1

environment lighting 36–39, *37–41*

FixedUpdate() functions 65
function(s)
    Awake() functions 65
    FixedUpdate() functions 65
    OnTriggerEnter() function 77
    of properties in unity **97–103**
    Start() function 65, 73, 75
    Update() functions 65

game engine
    comparison of different 5–7
    software 5
GameObject 7, *7*, 8, 67, 93
Global Illumination (GI) unity 15
graphic user interface (GUI) 13
    remotely operated vehicle (ROV)
        62–64, *63–64*

Hierarchy Window, ParticleSystem in
    41, *43*

joystick software installation 105–112,
    *105–112*

Kelpie **3**

light component
    properties for 51
    ROV 48
lighting, environment 36–39, *37–41*
light, properties of 101–102
light window (scene tab), properties of
    **98–100**

Manipulators script 71–72, *72*

Offshore Simulator Centre (OSC) 2, **2**
one-way ANOVA test 89
OnTriggerEnter() function 77

particles, underwater 40–42, *41–45*
ParticleSystem
    in Hierarchy Window 41, *43*
    in Unity3D 40
project creation 19, *20*

questionnaire 87, **88**, **89**, *90–92*

remotely operated vehicles (ROVs) 2
    add property in animation *53*
    animation window *54*
    box collider components *47*, *48*
    cameras settings for **49**, *50*
    capabilities for ROV simulators 1–2
    collider, properties **49**
    controller input 57–60, *58–61*, **60**, **61**
    data logging 62, *62*
    demand for 1
    gamification of ROV pilot training 5

remotely operated vehicles
        (ROVs) *(cont.)*
    graphic user interface (GUI) 62–64,
        *63–64*
    light component 48, **51**
    manipulators of 58
    model 13, 47, 48
        and specification 43–45,
            *45,* **46**
    pilot situational performance 87
    scripting 65, *65*
        ButtonScript 76–78, *77–79*
        CanvasScript.cs 135
        DataLogger 74–76, *75, 76*
        EmergencyLight.cs 134
        Grid.cs 113–114
        Heap.cs 115–116
        Manipulators 71–72, *72*
        Node.cs 117
        Pathfinding.cs 119–120
        PathRequestManager.cs 121
        Playerinput.cs 123–126
        PropellerMove.cs 133
        ROVARM.cs 132
        ROVCamera.cs 118
        ROVcollision.cs 131
        RovControl 65–69, *67, 68*
        Spotlight 73, *73*
        SwitchCamera 69–70, *70, 71*
        Timer 73–74, *74*
        UImainmenu.cs 130
        UIPlay.cs 130
        Underwater.cs 122
        Unit.cs 127–129
    simulators for, applications
        and features of different
        commercial **2–3**
    software structure 13–15, *14*
    spotlight GameObject for *51*
    spotlight settings for *52*
    TRV-M ROV 29
        box collider for *32*
        GameObject in Hierarchy
            View *51*
        import settings *30*
        properties of **46**
        in scene view *31*
        technical specification sheet *95*
    virtual *3*

remotely operated vehicles pilot
        simulator
    and ROVsim²Pro
        one-way ANOVA for proposed
            89, **89**
        t-test for comparing mean
            difference between proposed
            87, **88**
    user experience study 86
        participants 86
remotely operated vehicles pilot
        training
    report 84, **85**
    serious game-based virtual
        reality 89
    simulators 5
remotely operated vehicles, virtual
        environment development
        20–21, *21*
    environment lighting 36–39, *37–41*
    importing of subsea 3D models
        27–35, *29–37*
    underwater environment *38*
    underwater particles 40–42, *41–45*
    virtual seabed 21–27, *22–29*
        Terrain 22, *23*
        Terrain Collider 23
        transform 22
rigidbody
    component 47
    properties of **100–101**
RovControl script 65–69, *67, 68*
ROVs *see* remotely operated
        vehicles (ROVs)
ROVsim²Pro 3, 87, 93

Scene Gizmo 16, 17
scripts, remotely operated vehicle
        (ROV) 65, *65*
    ButtonScript 76–78, *77–79*
    CanvasScript.cs 135
    DataLogger 74–76, *75, 76*
    EmergencyLight.cs 134
    Grid.cs 113–114
    Heap.cs 115–116
    Manipulators 71–72, *72*
    Node.cs 117
    Pathfinding.cs 119–120
    PathRequestManager.cs 121

Playerinput.cs 123–126
PropellerMove.cs 133
ROVARM.cs 132
ROVCamera.cs 118
ROVcollision.cs 131
RovControl 65–69, *67, 68*
Spotlight 73, *73*
SwitchCamera 69–70, *70, 71*
Timer 73–74, *74*
UImainmenu.cs 130
UIPlay.cs 130
Underwater.cs 122
Unit.cs 127–129
serious games
    approach 4
    challenge-driven 4
    origin of 4
simulation
    test 81
    TRV-M configuration in virtual
        45–57, *46–48,* **49, 51**
simulators
    for ROVs 2–3
    ROVs pilot training 5
    underwater vehicle 2
    virtual 85
    VR 7
Spotlight script 73, *73*
Start() function 65, 73, 75
SwitchCamera script 69–70, *70, 71*

Terrain 21, 22, *23*
    height tool for 28
3D models, import settings for 32, **33**
3D game-making tool 5
3D ROV's environment 89
3D Virtual Operating Room project
        (3DVOR) 4
Timer script 73–74, *74*
TRV-M, configuration in virtual
        simulation 45–57, *46–48,*
        **49, 51**
TRV-M ROV 29
    box collider for *32*
    GameObject in Hierarchy
        View *51*
    import settings *30*
    properties of **46**
    in scene view *31*

technical specification sheet *95*
2D game-making tool 5

underwater particles 40–42, *41–45*
underwater vehicle simulators 2
unity
    configurations and setups 15
    functions of properties in **97–103**
    installation of 17–18, *18, 19*
    proposed methodology using 13, *14*
Unity3D 5, 6, 15
    framework, view *7,* 7–8
    game engine 4
    lighting window in 37
    ParticleSystem in 40
Unity 5 Editor 19
Unity™ Editor interface 15, *16,* 63
    hierarchy window 16
    inspector window 16
    project window 16
    scene view 15, 16
    toolbar 15–17
Unity's Global Illumination (GI) 15
Unreal Engine 6
Update() functions 65
UWSim **3**

vehicle simulators, underwater 2
videos, virtual simulation results with
        *81–84,* 81–85, **85**
virtual environment development,
        ROV 20–21, *21*
    environment lighting 36–39, *37–41*
    importing of subsea 3D models
        27–35, *29–37*
    underwater environment *38*
    underwater particles 40–42, *41–45*
    virtual seabed 21–27, *22–29*
        Terrain 22, *23*
        Terrain Collider 23
        transform 22
Virtual ROV **3**
virtual simulation
    results with videos *81–84,* 81–85, **85**
    TRV-M configuration in 45–57,
        *46–48,* **49, 51**
virtual simulator 85
VMAX ROV Simulator **3**
VR simulator 7

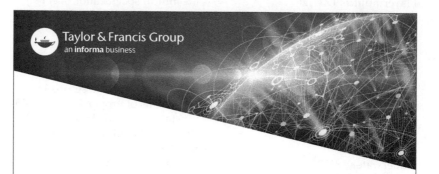